Social Security
What Every Human Services Professional Should Know

Victor L. Whiteman

Michigan State University

Best wishes,

Victor L. Whiteman

Allyn and Bacon

Boston • London • Toronto • Sydney • Tokyo • Singapore

Senior Series Editor: Judy Fifer
Series Editorial Assistant: Julianna Cancio
Senior Marketing Manager: Jackie Aaron
Production Administrator: Deborah Brown
Editorial-Production Coordinator: Marret Kauffner
Composition Buyer: Linda Cox
Manufacturing Buyer: Julie McNeill
Cover Administrator: Jenny Hart

Between the time Website information is gathered and then published, it is not unusual
for some sites to have closed. Also, the transcription of URLs can result in unintended
typographical errors. The publisher would appreciate notification where these occur so
that they may be corrected in subsequent editions. Thank you.

Library of Congress Cataloging-in-Publication Data
Whiteman, Victor L. (Victor Lee)
   Social security: what every human services professional should know /
Victor L. Whiteman.
      p. cm.
   ISBN 0-205-30790-6 (alk. paper)
      1. Social security. 2. Human services personnel--United States. I. Title.

HD7123 .W49 2000
368.4'3'00973--dc21   99-050146
                                                                     CIP

Printed in the United States of America

10 9 8 7 6 5 4 3 2 1   05 04 03 02 01 00

Contents

Preface

This book is written for human services professionals and other readers to provide them with an understanding of the importance and impact of the Social Security program on clients and society. It serves as a supplementary text for upper level undergraduate and graduate courses in social policy. It provides a reference for those who need information about the program's history, features, and future prospects.

Chapter 1 discusses the history of the Social Security program. Social workers and other human services professionals played an important role in the historical development of the program. These pioneers crafted the program to have a significant impact on the lives of their clientele. The Social Security program has been highly successful in meeting the original policy objectives, but now faces many challenges and obstacles.

The Social Security program's characteristics and provisions are documented in Chapters 2 and 3. Chapter 2 discusses retirement benefits, benefits to dependents, survivors benefits, disability benefits, and medical benefits. It provides details about eligibility for benefits and how to apply for them. Chapter 3 offers a description of the program's financial arrangements. The information in these chapters will be helpful for human services professionals in knowing when to refer their clients to the Social Security Administration and for enabling clients to receive the benefits to which they are entitled.

Chapters 4 through 7 assess the impact of the Social Security program on society. These chapters explore the program's impact on family structure and family life. They consider its impact on the poor in society. They analyze the question of whether women and minorities are treated with equity. Human services professionals need an understanding of these issues in order to have an informed point of view regarding needed changes in the Social Security program. Professionals can communicate these understandings to their clients in order to enable them to advocate for their own self interests.

The current Social Security program faces an upcoming financial crisis, as discussed in Chapters 8 and 9. This book provides a framework to assist readers in the development and analysis of proposals to avert this crisis. It summarizes a number of plans for resolving the potential crisis and assesses the policy implications of these plans. It suggests political strategies for promoting fair and adequate solutions to the financial problems of the Social Security program.

viii *Preface*

Thanks go to Dennis Preston of Preston Cartoon and Design in Lansing, Michigan, for drawing the final version of the book's cartoons and developing the images of the cartoon characters. The editorial assistance and support of my wife Jill greatly contributed to the successful completion of the book. The comments and materials provided by colleagues and students of the School of Social Work, Michigan State University, helped to shape and enhance the contents of the book. Thanks go to editors Judy Fifer and her staff and Marret Kauffner for their assistance in developing and publishing the book.

I would also like to thank the book's reviewers: Sue Jackson, Bloomsburg University; Robert B. Hudson, Boston University; Marcia B. Cohen, University of New England; and Michael Reisch, University of Pennsylvania.

Victor L. Whiteman

Chapter 1

Historical Development

A generation which ignores history has no past—and no future.
—Robert A. Heinlein

Social and Political Factors

The developers of the Social Security Act drew ideas from pre-existing pension and social insurance programs. The federal government created a public pension plan for United States war veterans after the Civil War. The federal civil service system provided retirement programs for employees. Most states provided school teachers with pension plans. Some states provided mandatory pension plans for some residents. Many city governments provided retired firemen and police officers with pensions (Popple & Leighninger 1998, p. 185).

Germany and England had previously developed national social insurance systems to insure people against risks of disability, illness, and unemployment. These programs spread the costs of dealing with such problems across a large number of people. They also redistributed income to some degree from the affluent to the needy. The ideas and models from pension and insurance programs in the United States and other countries were important politically for promoting the idea of social insurance and were used as a resource for development of the Social Security program.

Americans were slow to embrace the idea of social insurance. They endorsed values of self reliance, equitable distribution of goods according to effort, and local efforts to deal with problems of social dependence. These values did not lead to readily adopting a national social insurance system. It was not until the depression of 1929 that Americans began to consider social insurance as a potentially desirable alternative for dealing with economic insecurity.

1

Between 1929 and 1932 the value of stocks plummeted and the country's Gross National Product decreased by about one-third. Wages on average fell by half. Unemployment increased to more than 25 percent. Many banks and businesses failed. These phenomena led people to become increasingly aware that individual efforts were inadequate to deal with the economic problems of the country. Citizens began to seek and expect assistance from governmental bodies.

The depression had a particularly harsh impact upon the elderly. Many private pension plans ceased to exist. Private charities and relief agencies were unable to meet the demands of the elderly for assistance. The idea of some sort of government pension system became increasingly acceptable (Salisbury 1997, p. 31).

In the presidential election of 1932 Herbert Hoover ran on a platform of continuing private, nongovernmental intervention to deal with the problems of the depression. Franklin D. Roosevelt pledged to initiate governmental intervention and innovative approaches. The public clearly supported Roosevelt's strategy and elected him by a large margin. This gave President-elect Roosevelt a clear mandate to initiate new legislative efforts to deal with the economy.

Roosevelt took office in 1933 and immediately began taking action to cope with the country's economic crisis. His first efforts were to develop temporary relief measures such as the Federal Emergency Relief Administration (FERA). Roosevelt viewed such efforts as temporary approaches to the economic problems of the country. He considered jobs as more important than handouts, and created public work programs that both provided jobs and developed the country's economic infrastructure (Popple & Leighninger 1998, p. 186).

President Roosevelt established a Committee on Economic Security in 1934 to develop legislation to respond to the economic crisis in a long-term preventive approach through the use of social insurance programs. Francis Perkins, who was Secretary of Labor and a social worker, chaired the committee. Another social worker, Harry Hopkins, the administrator of the Federal Emergency Relief Program, was also a member of the Committee on Economic Security. The committee included a broad representation of academics and government officials. It did much of the actual formulation of legislation for the Social Security Act.

Proposed legislation termed the Townsend Plan played a significant role in promoting the need to provide governmental income security for the aged. The plan was named after a California doctor who proposed monthly checks of $200 for each retired man or woman more than 60 years of age. In order to receive benefits, the plan required that recipients spend all of the money within a 30-day period. Townsend believed that the economy could be rejuvenated by initiating consumer consumption. This plan promised to both deal with the poverty of the elderly and to help in spending our way out of the recession.

Townsend proposed a 2 percent business transaction tax in order to finance the plan. Although his plan met with some unfavorable responses, he developed a large constituency of supporters. His supporters submitted a petition signed by 20 million people giving strong support to passage of the Townsend Plan. Although the Roosevelt administration did not adopt this plan, it influenced the development of the old age insurance program of the Social Security Act (Salisbury 1997, p. 32).

Social work organizations and labor unions pressured the government to develop programs to deal with unemployment. These groups and their supporters wanted legislation that would support unemployed workers who were seeking jobs. The organizations were also strong supporters of programs to provide pensions for elderly people.

The Roosevelt administration wanted to develop permanent and ongoing programs to give the nation a strong economic foundation in order to avoid further social trauma. Roosevelt believed that this could best be accomplished through a single piece of legislation that established the needed social insurance and public welfare programs. This approach allowed certain controversial programs to be bundled with programs that were more popular and had more political support. Programs such as unemployment insurance might not pass unless coupled with more popular programs such as old age pensions (Jansson 1997, p. 173).

In the 1930s social workers generally supported the Roosevelt administration and its policies. They held a variety of political opinions ranging from the extremely conservative to the socialistic and communistic. Most social workers believed that the federal government should be involved in funding and delivering economic and social services to needy people. Social workers generally considered themselves to be a part of the broad coalition that supported the new deal. Many social workers were somewhat perplexed, however, by the conservative attitudes and values reflected in some of Roosevelt's policy decisions. For example, his decision to terminate the Civilian Works Administration, which funded local improvement projects, displeased many social workers. The social work community also tended to be critical of the low benefit levels given to the financially needy as provided by the Federal Emergency Relief Administration. Many social workers were politically prominent during the early 1930s, and the profession exerted pressure to develop legislation that was compatible with its political agenda. The New Deal reflected many of the ideas and positions of the social work profession (Jansson 1997, pp. 192–193).

Policy Objectives

The policy objectives of the Social Security Act revolved around providing economic security for those in an industrial society facing the predictable problems of old age, unemployment, and disability. President Roosevelt was also concerned about health care, but decided to postpone addressing this issue until a later date. The framers of the Social Security program lacked a clear consensus about program features that would accomplish these goals. Their concern about issues of both adequacy and equity seems clear from the final legislation. The principle of adequacy affirms the desirability of providing assistance to poor people to meet their basic needs. The adequacy principle tends to promote social policies that redistribute income such as welfare programs. The principle of equity asserts that people should receive benefits based on their contributions. The equity principle tends to promote social policies that do not redistribute income. The 1935 Social Security Act promoted adequacy through economic redistribution provisions as reflected in both the social insurance and public assistance programs. The act reflected the principle of equity in the social insurance program provisions that linked benefit amounts to the size of contribution (Achenbaum 1986, pp. 3–4).

President Roosevelt viewed relief programs such as the FERA as meeting temporary needs. He wanted to develop programs that went beyond meeting temporary problems and would provide a sustained basis for promoting economic security in the US. Roosevelt believed that unemployment and economic insecurity undermined a stable democratic society. He used his leadership to promote social programs that would be stable and productive in promoting long-term economic stability.

In June 1934 President Roosevelt urged Congress to develop and pass social legislation that would promote economic security and protect members of society from economic problems associated with old age and unemployment. He indicated that in January 1935 he would propose a program to accomplish these goals. The Committee on Economic Security (CES) was charged by President Roosevelt to develop a proposal that would protect the economic security of men, women, and children. The president's objectives included those of providing decent housing for all people, to increase employment opportunities through the development of the nation's natural resources, and to protect against life's hazards and misfortunes. The committee was to accomplish this through the development of social insurance programs for working people and public assistance programs for those who were unemployable. The programs were to be developed so that all citizens would have access to a decent standard of food, clothing, and housing (Salisbury 1997, p. 32).

President Roosevelt did not support the Townsend Plan. He considered this plan to be financially untenable. It called for a flat benefit structure unrelated to contributions or need, and Roosevelt believed that benefits needed to be related to an individual's contributions. The Townsend Plan had a good deal of political support, and Roosevelt wanted the committee to quickly develop program proposals that were more compatible with his political viewpoints.

The CES approached its task by focusing on economic security plans that had been implemented in the states of Ohio and Wisconsin. The Ohio plan provided a living wage for needy unemployed or retired individuals. It involved a public welfare approach for promoting economic security. The Wisconsin plan emphasized a preventive approach for promoting economic security. It linked benefits to a person's wage and work history. This supported the values related to the American work ethic and the principle of equity. Under the Wisconsin plan the achievements in a person's past served as a basis for protection from economic insecurity when a man or woman became elderly or disabled.

Roosevelt clearly favored the Wisconsin plan. In appointing the CES he selected a majority of members who supported it. Roosevelt wanted an approach to economic security that reflected the value of the work ethic and that would be distinct from a public welfare program. He viewed public welfare programs as primarily temporary measures to be used in times of crisis. Longer term preventive programs needed to be developed that promoted work and individual effort as a basis for benefits. Roosevelt favored a social insurance approach for dealing with the problems of old age and unemployment. He believed this approach was politically acceptable to a majority of Americans. Social insurance programs also had the potential for reducing the number of people receiving welfare (Salisbury 1997, p. 33).

Reduction of social turmoil appears to be one of the major goals for developing the social insurance programs. Those favoring the provision of social insurance thought that old age insurance would allow older men and women to retire and become consumers. It was thought that both the retirement and the consumerism of older workers would create new jobs and spur economic growth. The passage of social insurance was seen as a form of remedial action that would

U.S. SCALE OF SOCIAL

quell labor unrest. Roosevelt found such arguments to be in congruence with his philosophy of recovery through employment rather than welfare relief (Salisbury 1997, p. 38).

President Roosevelt supported the idea of a self financed old age insurance program. This plan called for placing payroll taxes in a trust fund to be retained there for payment of benefits to the contributors when needed. He believed such a program would be politically secure and that contributory financing would give individuals a sense of entitlement to benefits. Roosevelt's plan was opposed by those who thought that economic growth might be stunted by creating a huge reserve fund. There was also concern that employers would pass the full cost of taxation to employees by lowering their wages or charging higher prices for their products. Opponents proposed that people with low incomes be exempted from the payroll tax or that old age insurance be financed through general tax revenues, with increased taxes for business and the wealthy. In spite of such opposition, Congress adopted the president's plan (Altmeyer 1966, pp. 11, 34).

Passage of the Social Security Act

A final report from the CES was issued in January 1935. The legislative bill based on the CES report included both social insurance programs and public welfare programs. The legislation provided for old age insurance and unemployment insurance. It proposed public assistance for the aged, for dependent children in single-parent families, for disabled children, and for the blind. The bill provided federal funds for public health work. The legislation passed and became law in August 1935.

The legislation provided for self-funding of the social insurance programs through payroll taxes. The initial tax was 2 percent of an employee's first $3,000 of wages with the employer and employee each paying 1 percent. This avoided using general revenue funds, which would have given the programs the appearance of being welfare programs. The use of payroll taxes made it more difficult for Congress to dismantle the social insurance programs by not including funding for them through general revenue taxes. In contrast, the 1935 act did fund welfare programs through general revenue taxes. These programs were designed to help the deserving poor who were elderly or the children in a home with a missing parent.

The Social Security program honored states' rights by giving the federal government relatively little control over the public welfare programs. In addition, each state developed its own plan for unemployment compensation. However, the old age insurance program broke away from the tradition of state control by establishing a federally administered and controlled social program.

The old age insurance program was the feature of the Social Security bill that drew the most criticism in Congress. It was viewed as a program that detracted from the private market system. Opponents of the bill were concerned about hurting American industry through new forms of taxation. They charged that the bill would develop a large federal bureaucracy to provide insurance that could be more appropriately provided by private industry. These arguments, however, were not sufficient to defeat the Social Security bill. Both the House and Senate passed the bill by a wide margin. The passage of the Social Security Act constituted a major change in the approach to social welfare in the United States (Altmeyer 1966, pp. 32–33, 37–42).

Program Implementation

The controversy concerning the Social Security Act did not stop after it was adopted. Some believed that the act was too socialistic and radical. The U.S. Chamber of Commerce and the National Association of Manufacturers opposed the Social Security Act for such reasons. These organizations took the position that the act did not uphold the values of American society that stress individual liberty and self-responsibility (Trattner 1989, p. 265).

Other voices such as Frank J. Bruno, a noted social work educator, criticized the act as being far too conservative. Critics pointed out that insurance benefits would not provide adequate standard of living for those who were totally dependent on it. They noted that the tax was regressive because low wage earners paid a higher percentage of their income in taxes than did high wage earners. Critics asserted that the bill was deflationary and deprived workers of needed purchasing power (Trattner 1989, p. 265).

In 1937 the Supreme Court confirmed the constitutionality of the Social Security Act in two separate decisions. In the decision concerning *Steward Machine Co. v. Davis* the court validated the collection of unemployment insurance tax from employers of eight or more employees. They ruled such collections to be constitutional because they promoted the general welfare. The court legitimized the use of payroll taxes to provide old age insurance benefits in the case of *Helvering v. Davis*. It held that in an increasingly industrialized society the elderly were adversely affected in terms of job and wage discrimination.

Legislation passed in 1939 that broadened the Social Security program to include family members of workers. The new legislation gave protection to a retired or surviving worker's wife, children, and dependent aged parents. These revisions meant that married beneficiaries would receive larger payments than would single beneficiaries with equal levels of contributions. The legislation promoted the economic security of families and family stability. Critics asserted that the legislation reflected a patriarchal view of the family, which ideally contained a male worker and a dependent family (Abramovitz 1988, p. 254).

The 1939 legislation advanced the first pension payments from 1942 to 1940. The amendments modified the retirement test for receiving old age insurance benefits by allowing beneficiaries to earn up to $15 per month from insurance-covered employment. They increased projected benefit amounts by basing benefits on average rather than total wages. The legislation rescinded the scheduled increase in total worker-employer taxes and maintained a 2 percent tax rate. Until 1939 workers paid benefits into a reserve fund, which was to be used to later pay benefits to these contributors. The government bought bonds with surpluses from the reserve fund to finance current operations. This act introduced pay-as-you-go financing, allowing the payments of current contributors to be used to fund payments to current beneficiaries.

Congress passed the 1939 amendments in the face of increasing discontent with a program that was not scheduled to pay benefits until 1942. Workers were paying into the program and not receiving any immediate benefits. They had reduced purchasing power due to Social Security taxes, and this was perceived by many to be detrimental to their own welfare and the currently depressed economy.

Groups representing the elderly lobbied for broader and more immediate coverage. This lobbying effort was largely promoted by those who were a part of the Townsend movement. The 1939 amendments laid a foundation for inadequate long-term financing, but met the current political pressure to revise and liberalize the system. Future generations were subjected to the possibility of paying significantly increased taxes to meet benefit claims. The 1939 amendments that introduced additional family benefits without additional contributions made a significant change in the nature of social insurance in the United States. These amendments weakened the insurance principle of linking benefit levels directly to contribution levels. This moved the program away from the approach of giving benefits based on the value of equity and toward the approach of giving benefits based on the value of adequacy (Abramovitz 1988, p. 254).

In the 1940s public welfare provided more benefits to more beneficiaries than did the social insurance programs. Interest in social insurance declined, and politicians questioned the need for such programs. Congress repeatedly canceled scheduled increases in Social Security tax rates based on their judgment that there was little need for program expansion. Congress defeated scheduled increases in Social Security taxes in 1943, 1946, and 1949. Many congressional representatives believed that means-tested programs provided adequate old age security.

Strengthening the Social Security System

The Social Security advisory council issued several reports in 1948 recommending strengthening Social Security as a means of preventing dependency and reducing the need for public welfare. The council argued that Social Security linked benefits to contributions, which made it preferable to public welfare approaches for promoting economic security. A number of labor unions lobbied for expansion of the Social Security program since their private pension benefits were linked to old age insurance benefits. There was political pressure to expand and revise the Social Security system.

A bill passed in 1950 brought the benefit level of old age insurance to a parity with the welfare provisions of old age assistance. The 1950 amendments increased old age insurance benefits by 77 percent. Congress raised the employer-employee tax rate to 3 percent and scheduled future increases to a maximum rate of 6.5 percent to be paid in 1970. They increased the taxable wage base from $3,000 to $3,600.

The 1950 act added most urban (nonfarm) self-employed individuals to the Social Security system. Some professional self-employed individuals were excluded. Self-employed individuals paid Social Security taxes as a part of the process of filing income tax returns. Regularly employed agricultural and domestic workers were added to the system. Employees of nonprofit organizations and many state and local government employees were made eligible for coverage on a voluntary basis. These changes increased the importance of the social insurance programs in comparison to public welfare programs. The Social Security insurance programs began to increase in popularity with the general public (Cohen 1960, pp. 83–84).

The 1950 amendments moved the Social Security program away from the insurance principle of basing benefits on contributions. The amendments reduced the quarters of coverage required to become eligible for benefits and increased the benefits payable to those with short periods of coverage. However, the reductions were transitory because requirements for quarters of coverage were scheduled to increase over time (Burns 1956, pp. 29–31).

After passage of the 1950 amendments the number of people receiving old age insurance quickly passed the number of people receiving old age assistance. In 1951 for the first-time total old age insurance benefits surpassed the total benefit amounts for old age assistance. In 1953 Social Security coverage was extended to self-employed farmers and other previously excluded agricultural and domestic workers. Additional groups of state and local government employees were made eligible for coverage. The 1953 amendments raised average Social Security benefits by 13 percent. They increased the maximum wage on which taxes would be paid to $4,200, and retained the scheduled employer-employee tax rate increase to 4 percent. In 1956 legislation passed to add coverage on a permanent contributory basis for individuals serving in the military services (Cohen 1960, pp. 83–84).

Disability Insurance

Congress passed a disability Social Security insurance program in 1956. The passage and administration of disability insurance posed a number of difficulties that were not faced by other insurance programs. Actuaries thought that predicting the future cost of such a program was extremely difficult. Disability is an elusive concept that is difficult to define. Administrators faced the problem of developing criteria to determine the work capability of applicants (Kingson & Schulz 1997, p. 31).

Prior to the 1956 disability insurance program, the United States had very limited involvement in providing such coverage. The 1938 Railroad Unemployment Insurance Act provided a national program that covered temporary disability for railroad workers. The act provided coverage for loss of wages only and did not cover medical costs. It was financed through a payroll tax levied on employers. In the 1940s California, New Jersey, and Rhode Island established temporary disability insurance programs for covered workers (Burns 1949, pp. 209–210, 251–257).

The Eisenhower administration did not favor the creation of disability insurance. A number of concessions were made in order to get the bill signed into law. The law provided for a separate disability insurance trust fund so that the program could be closely monitored. Disability determinations were to be made by state offices working on a contractual basis. Most states attempted to link disability benefits with rehabilitation efforts by placing disability determination services in the hands of the same bureaucracies that administered vocational rehabilitation programs. The legislation limited disability benefits to men and women more than 50 years of age and did not extend benefits to dependents. It stated that a person must have a medical impairment that will result in death, or that will continue indefinitely, to receive benefits.

Wilbur Mills, the chairman of the Ways and Means Committee, introduced legislation in 1958 to raise Social Security benefits by 7 percent. Congress passed this increase and also extended benefits to dependents of disabled Social Security beneficiaries that year. In 1960 Congress eliminated the age 50 requirement for receiving Social Security disability coverage, making men and women of all ages eligible.

Health Insurance

In the 1960s there was rekindled debate about the need for some type of national health insurance in the United States. Senator John F. Kennedy made health insurance for the elderly a key presidential campaign issue in 1960. Advocates for national health insurance emphasized the connections between poverty and poor health. During the presidential race Congress enacted a limited form of medical assistance for elderly welfare recipients called Medical Aid for the Elderly. It provided grants-in-aid for the states to develop medical programs for elderly welfare recipients (Popple & Leighninger 1998, p. 255).

The political climate and value system in the United States supported only a limited approach to national health insurance. A program with comprehensive coverage was not given serious consideration. Opponents such as the American Medical Association feared that the country was moving toward a system of socialized medicine. To enhance political acceptability, proposals for national health insurance had to be restricted to programs for people with low-income and the elderly who had limited access to medical care in the current private health care system. Supporters of health insurance had to develop proposals that would be acceptable to most health care providers, consumers, and private employers.

President Lyndon Johnson supported health insurance for Social Security beneficiaries as a part of the War on Poverty. The Social Security Administration structured the proposal for Medicare to carefully limit governmental involvement in providing health care services. They proposed legislation that allowed hospitals to transact business with private insurance agencies such as Blue Cross. The proposal avoided governmental development of medical fee schedules. It set no limits on the fees charged by hospitals or physicians. The resulting program, when passed, was one of federal funding with private control of costs (Popple & Leighninger 1998, p. 256).

In 1965 Congress passed Medicare as Title XVIII of the Social Security Act to provide medical insurance for recipients of old age insurance benefits. The legislation established hospital insurance through Part A of Medicare. This feature of Medicare found political legitimization through the argument that such benefits were earned by beneficiaries by tax contributions based on their earnings. The legislation established Part B to provide supplementary medical insurance for doctors' bills. Part B coverage gained political acceptance by being voluntary and paid for in part by beneficiaries.

Congress passed Medicaid as Title XIX of the Social Security Act to provide medical benefits to welfare recipients. This act provided a broad range of medical assistance to those eligible for welfare. It conformed to a politically acceptable principle of providing needed assistance only for the impoverished.

The 1965 legislation also changed other aspects of the Social Security system. It raised the earnings base on which Social Security taxes were paid and increased Social Security benefits by 7 percent. Although the combined employer-employee Social Security tax rate was to have been 8.25 percent in 1966, the 1965 act reduced that rate to 7.7 percent. An additional tax was then added to support the Medicare program, bringing the total tax rate to 8.4 percent. The legislation changed wage restrictions to allow for increased earnings for Social Security beneficiaries without losing benefits. It created a more liberal definition of disability and instituted rehabilitation services for recipients of disability insurance. The act expanded the scope of childhood disability benefits. It lowered the age at which widows could receive benefits.

In 1983 Medicare was altered by introducing a system of national payment levels related to what was termed as diagnostic related groups or DRGs. The Medicare program experienced rapid increases in expenditures after its inception in 1965. To remedy this situation the Reagan administration proposed that there be set payment levels to hospitals for treatment of people with a particular diagnosis. Except for unusual situations, hospitals received the prescribed set fee regardless of the time that a person stayed in the hospital. Later legislation in 1989 established a similar system for doctors' fees.

Trust Fund Crisis

In 1969 Congress raised benefits for Social Security recipients by 15 percent. They raised benefits for Social Security recipients another 20 percent in 1972 and 11 percent in 1974. In addition to raising benefits, the 1972 legislation provided Medicare coverage for those with an end-stage renal disease. It allowed Medicare coverage for disability beneficiaries after a two-year waiting period.

The 1972 legislation provided a new plan for increasing Social Security benefits. It instituted automatic annual cost-of-living adjustments beginning in

1975. The legislation assumed that wages as well as payroll taxes would continue to rise in tandem in the future. The cost of living adjustments, or COLA, would automatically keep benefit levels aligned with current economic conditions (Achenbaum 1986, p. 250).

In 1977 prices were rising faster than wages, creating problems in the Social Security system due to the cost-of-living adjustments. Benefit levels were increasing at a more rapid rate than Social Security taxes. Congress passed corrective legislation that increased taxes and increased the wage base that was subject to Social Security taxation. This action, however, did not solve the problem of financing the Social Security program. The economy continued to worsen, with inflation rising faster than wages. The balance of funds in the Old Age and Survivors Trust Fund continued to decline, with the possibility that funds in 1983 would not be sufficient to pay the benefits due Social Security beneficiaries. President Reagan created the Greenspan Commission to deal with this crisis.

Based on recommendations by the Greenspan Commission, Congress passed legislation in 1983 to increase future payroll taxes to a combined employer-employee rate of 14 percent. The act increased the tax rate on self-employed people so that it would rise over time to be double that of the rate for individuals. The legislation increased the maximum wage base on which Social Security taxes were paid to $37,800, and future increases were made dependent on the economy. The act added an income tax on up to one-half of the Social Security benefits received by recipients whose taxable income plus one-half of their Social Security payments exceeded $25,000 for an individual or $32,000 for a couple. Proceeds from these income taxes were to be transferred to the Social Security trust funds.

The 1983 legislation delayed cost-of-living increases by six months. The six-month delay represented a permanent decrease in benefits that was not scheduled to be made up at a later date. The act modified the method of determining cost-of-living increases when the resources in the trust fund fall below 20 percent of the expected outlay for the year. Under those circumstances either the Consumer Price Index or the average wage increase, whichever is less, would be used to determine cost-of-living increases.

The 1983 act expanded coverage of the Social Security program to additional federal, state, and local governmental employees. It also added coverage for more self-employed workers and all employees of nonprofit organizations. The legislation raised the normal retirement age to 67 years as phased in gradually over a 24-year period beginning in 2003. It authorized future reductions in benefits for those retiring at age 62 from 80 percent to 70 percent of the amount that they would receive when retiring at full retirement age. These legislative changes provided an immediate increase in the balance of the Old Age and Survivors Trust Fund. They produced temporary fund adequacy, but failed to procure a permanent solution for fund stability.

For retired workers there recently has been some easing of the rules that penalize part-time work. The earnings that a retired person less than 70 years of age can have without reducing Social Security benefits will gradually rise to $30,000 by the year 2002. Individuals more than 70 years of age can continue to earn unlimited wage amounts without losing Social Security benefits.

References

Abramovitz, M. 1988. *Regulating the Lives of Women*. Boston: South End Press.

Achenbaum, W. A. 1986. *Social Security: Visions and Revisions*. New York: Cambridge University Press.

Altmeyer, A. J. 1966. *The Formative Years of Social Security*. Madison: University of Wisconsin Press.

Burns, E. M. 1949. *The American Social Security System*. New York: Houghton Mifflin Company.

———. 1956. *Social Security and Public Policy*. New York: McGraw-Hill.

Cohen, W. J. 1960. "Twenty-Five Years of Progress in Social Security." In W. Haber & W. J. Cohen (Eds.), *Social Security Programs, Problems, and Policies* . Homewood, IL: Richard D. Irwin, Inc.

Jansson, B. S. 1997. *The Reluctant Welfare State American Social Welfare Policies—Past, Present, and Future*. (3rd ed.). Pacific Grove, CA: Brooks/Cole Publishing Company.

Kingson, E. R., & Schulz, J. H. 1997. "Should Social Security Be Means Tested?" In E. R. Kingson & J. H. Schulz (Eds.), *Social Security in the 21st Century*. New York: Oxford University Press.

Popple, P. R., & Leighninger, L. 1998. *The Policy-Based Profession: An Introduction to Social Welfare Policy for Social Workers*. Needham Heights, MA: Allyn & Bacon.

Salisbury, D. L. 1997. *Assessing Social Security Reform Alternatives*. Washington, DC: Employee Benefit Research Institute.

Trattner, W. I. 1989. *From Poor Law to Welfare State: A History of Social Welfare in America*. (4th ed.). New York: The Free Press.

Chapter 2

Processes and Benefits

Anyone who isn't confused really doesn't understand the situation.
—Edward R. Murrow

Program Features

The Social Security program includes old age, survivors, disability, and health insurance and has an acronym of OASDHI. Some authors call the program RSDHI, standing for retirement, survivors, disability, and health insurance. The most common acronym is OASDHI, but in the future RSDHI may become the accepted nomenclature (Landis 1993, p. 8).

OASDHI is the nation's largest social program, covering approximately nine out of ten employees. Eligible retiring workers and their dependent family members receive monthly benefit payments. On the death of an insured worker a lump sum benefit is paid to the worker's eligible spouse or children. The program pays monthly benefits to dependent survivors of insured employees and to eligible disabled persons and their dependents. Covered disabled individuals and those 65 years of age and over receive Medicare benefits.

Approximately 44 million individuals receive monthly Social Security checks. Those receiving benefits include 31 million retired workers, spouses, and children; 7 million survivors of deceased workers; and 6 million disabled workers, spouses, and children. The Social Security Administration receives about 34,000 claims per day and more than 12 million claims each year.

People may obtain information about their Social Security status by requesting and completing form SSA-7004. This form may be obtained from any

16

Social Security office, by downloading it from the web site at www.ssa.gov, or by calling 1-800-772-1213. The form asks individuals to give their latest current earnings and to estimate their future earnings. It asks for an estimated future retirement date. Submitting multiple forms with different estimates is acceptable and sometimes desirable. Information will be returned about each form submitted, giving estimates of future benefits. It is important that everyone periodically obtain a personal statement of his or her Social Security status to make sure that records have been correctly recorded and to use this information in planning for future benefits.

The benefit statement will give information about the number of Social Security work credits on the person's record and the number of credits that are still needed to become eligible for program benefits. It will show a person's total Social Security earnings and the Federal Insurance Contributions Act (FICA) taxes paid on them between 1937 and 1950, and provide a year-by-year record of earnings and taxes paid from 1951 to the present time. The report will show the maximum yearly earnings subject to Social Security tax in each of these periods. It will estimate retirement benefits when retiring at a reported planned retirement age, at full retirement age, and at age 70. It will also provide estimated survivors benefits and disability benefits.

Application for Benefits

To obtain benefits from the Social Security program applicants need to file a claim. Claims may be filed by visiting a local Social Security office or over the phone by calling 1-800-772-1213. A claims representative will assist an applicant in obtaining needed information and documentation. The representative will explain the options that are available and the consequences of choosing each option.

Individuals applying for Social Security need to know their Social Security number, date of birth, recent wage history, and names of current and former spouses and children. They must provide information about government, military, or railroad work history. Applicants need to supply documentation that gives proof of age, marital status, and recent wage history. Applicants for survivors benefits need to furnish a death certificate. Records of military service or other public pensions are needed if applicable. Applicants receive either a letter showing an award or a letter indicating denial of the application.

Claims need to be filed before the date of expected benefits. Claims for retirement and family benefits should be filed three or four months before their expected receipt. A survivor's claim should be filed during the month of death when recipients are immediately eligible for benefits or, if not immediately eligible, three or four months before becoming eligible for benefits. Disability claims should be filed immediately, if possible, after a person becomes disabled and not later than 18 months after the occurrence of disability.

Appeals Process

Social Security applicants or recipients who are dissatisfied with the decisions made by the Social Security Administration can usually appeal. They must appeal within 60 days after receiving written notification of a decision. If a person files an appeal after 60 days have passed, the Social Security Administration may or may not agree to consider it. A person can appeal decisions concerning a denied benefit claim, the amount of benefits to be paid, adjustments in benefits, recorded earnings, deductions from benefits, termination of benefits, and other related issues. He or she cannot appeal the fee set by the Social Security Administration to pay an attorney to represent an applicant or a decision to disqualify a person from representing an applicant. He or she also cannot appeal a decision to deny an extension of time to file a report of earnings or a decision to withhold part of a person's monthly payment to recover past overpayments (Landis 1993, p. 164).

People who are dissatisfied may be able to resolve problems without a formal appeal. They should discuss problems with a Social Security representative to clarify the decisions made and the basis for those decisions. If an error has been made, the Social Security representative can often make corrections. If problems cannot be resolved in this manner, a person may appeal. The first step in an appeal process is called a reconsideration. A person must make a written request for a reconsideration by completing the proper form. The reconsideration form asks for an explanation of the disagreement. It must be signed and submitted to the Social Security Administration. An appellant can present evidence to support his or her position. The Social Security representative assigned to review the problem will be someone other than the original representative. He or she will consider available information and make a new, but not necessarily different determination. The new determination is not limited to the points of disagreement and may include other corrections or changes. Someone not satisfied with the result of the reconsideration may appeal in writing within 60 days after he or she receives notice of the decision (Landis 1993, p. 165).

The Social Security Administration reviews an appeal of a reconsideration through a hearing. An administrative law judge, who works for the Social Security Administration, will preside at the hearing. The judge will review the appealed case and consider any relevant additional information the appellant wants to present. Appellants may appoint a qualified representative to help them in presenting their case. They may call witnesses to support their case. The judge may request information of various kinds from the appellant or ask for expert opinion regarding various issues. The judge will make a determination in the case and written notice will be sent to the appellant. This determination may be appealed in writing within 60 days (Landis 1993, pp. 165–166).

A final level of appeal within the Social Security Administration is a review by the Appeals Council held in Washington, D.C. Appellants can provide information in writing, but they cannot attend this review. The Appeals Council has the authority to make decisions only about whether proper procedures were followed during the hearing. It will not revise the decisions made. If the Appeals Council decides that the procedures were improper, the judge of the hearing will be asked to reconsider the decision. In such cases the procedures may be corrected or the decision may be changed. If appellants are not satisfied with the decision, they can appeal it in a federal District Court within a 60-day period after they receive notice of the outcome (Landis 1993, p. 167).

Taxation of Benefits

Cash benefits paid to social security beneficiaries may be subject to income tax. The taxation of cash benefits is based on the 1983 Social Security amendments and the deficit reduction legislation enacted in 1993. When adjusted gross income, tax-free interest income, and one-half of Old Age, Survivors, and Disability Insurance (OASDI) cash benefits total between $25,000 and $34,000 for a single-income tax payer, up to 50 percent of Social Security income is subject to income tax. Single persons are subject to the taxation of 85 percent of Social Security benefits when such income totals $34,000 or more. If this total is between $32,000 and $44,000 for a couple filing a joint return, up to 50 percent of Social Security income is subject to income tax. Couples filing a joint return are subject to the taxation of up to 85 percent of Social Security benefits when such income totals $44,000 or more. Rules governing the taxation of Social Security benefits do not include provisions to index for inflation. In the future an increasing proportion of recipients will pay taxes on their Social Security benefits.

Retirement Benefits

Eligibility

To receive retirement benefits a person must be 62 years of age or older. Individuals must be 65 years of age or older to receive full retirement benefits. The age for receiving full retirement benefits will gradually increase to age 67 in the future.

To receive retirement benefits a person's earnings must be low enough to demonstrate retirement if they are less than 70 years of age. The earnings test or retirement test does not count income from dividends, interest, rents, pensions, annuity payments, or other types of investment income. It does count gross wages from employment. It counts earnings from self-employment and hours of work in self-employment. Special rules apply to assessing the worth of work from self-employment. Special rules apply to the initial retirement year so that earnings in the months before retirement are excluded from consideration.

When beneficiaries are below age 65, regulations require that benefits be reduced by $1.00 for every $2.00 earned above a specified amount of earnings allowed without benefit reduction. Beneficiaries between 65 and 69 years of age have benefits reduced by $1.00 for every $3.00 above a specified amount of earnings. The level of earnings not subject to benefit reduction for individuals below 65 years of age is $9,120 (1998). For individuals 65 to 69 years of age, the earnings level not subject to benefit reduction is $14,500 (1998). The amount of exemptions for beneficiaries less than 65 years of age is indexed to change with the growth in average wages. Earnings not subject to benefit reduction will gradually rise to $30,000 by the year 2002 for retirees 65 to 69 years of age. The exempt amounts for beneficiaries 65 to 69 years of age will be indexed to change with growth in average wages after the year 2002. Retirees 70 years of age or more may have unlimited earnings without reduction of benefits.

To be eligible for retirement benefits a person must have 40 work credits if he or she was born in 1929 or later. One work credit less per earlier birth year is required for people born before 1929. Before 1978 a work credit was given for each calendar quarter in which a person paid 50 dollars or more in Social Security insurance premiums. People currently receive one work credit for each $700 (1998) of earnings on which Social Security insurance premiums are paid during a given year. Most people who are employed pay FICA (Federal Insurance Contributions Act) taxes that are automatically withdrawn from their paychecks. A few federal and local civil service employees are not a part of the Social Security system. People who are self-employed pay FICA taxes when filing their income tax. Those people with employment in both a foreign country and in the United States can combine work credits into one system when there are international agreements between the two countries. Those people who do not have 40 work credits themselves may be eligible for retirement benefits based on the employment record of their spouse or in some circumstances their former spouse (Social Security Administration 1998, p. 29).

Benefits

A complex set of factors including lifetime average earnings, age of retirement, and inflation factors determine the cash benefits that a person receives. Before other computations a person's wages are adjusted for inflation. The inflation adjustment converts nonrecent wages to the equivalent value of wages earned in the year that the applicant turned 60 years of age. For individuals who become disabled or who die, the wages are adjusted to two years before that event. Earnings after these times are counted at their nominal value. The Social Security Administration determines the inflation adjustment by the changes in average wages reported to it. Due to a continuous cap on the amount of earnings that can be reported to the Social Security Administration, the inflation adjustment does not fully reflect the effects of wage inflation. Recent wages are typically the highest even after the inflation factor has been computed for past wages. People retiring early sometimes omit periods of what would have been their highest wages in determining Social Security retirement benefits. Often such omissions result in a minor rather than major reduction of Social Security benefits, but considering this factor in planning for retirement is useful.

The Administration uses inflation-adjusted wages to calculate a person's lifetime average earnings. It bases lifetime average earnings, for those retiring, on their highest 35 years of wages. When people have careers lasting longer than 35 years on which they paid Social Security taxes, the lowest earnings years are dropped out of the computation. Individuals retiring who have paid Social Security taxes in fewer than 35 years will have years with zero earnings added into the computation. The Administration bases computations on fewer years for retiring individuals born before 1929. It includes one year less in the average for each year of birth before 1929. People who die or become disabled have fewer years of earnings included in the computation. Wages for the highest 35 years (or less) of earnings are summed and divided by the number of months in those years. This calculation produces the Average Indexed Monthly Earnings, or AIME (Steuerle & Bakija 1994, p. 76).

The Administration uses AIME to compute the primary insurance amount, or PIA. The PIA is the monthly benefit amount payable to a worker who retires at age 65. To calculate the non-inflation-adjusted PIA multiply the first $477 (1998) of AIME by 90 percent. Multiply the next $2,398 (1998) of AIME by 32 percent. Multiply any amount of AIME above $2,875 (1998) by 15 percent. The dollar amounts used in the calculation, in this case $477 and $2,875, are called bend points. The Administration adjusts them annually to account for inflation. The bend points used in a calculation are those that are in effect at the time that person becomes 62 year years old, becomes disabled, or dies. The percentage multipliers remain constant from year to year. This method of calculation provides a higher proportion of return on AIME for low-wage earners than for high wage earners. The Administration refers to the percentage return on AIME as a replacement rate. Retirees with very low average earnings have a replacement rate of up to 90 percent. Retirees with average wages have a replacement rate of approximately 40 percent of AIME. Very high earners have a replacement rate of approximately 34 percent of their average earnings (Social Security Administration 1998, p. 36)

Using the bend points a person with an AIME of $3,000 would have a non-inflation-adjusted PIA of $1,215.41, calculated as follows:

$$1. \ \$477 \times .90 \quad = \$\,429.30$$
$$2. \ \$2,398 \times .32 \ = \$\,767.36$$
$$3. \ \$125 \times .15 \quad = \underline{\$\ \ 18.75}$$

$$\text{PIA} \quad = \$1,215.41$$

The Administration makes cost-of-living adjustments after a person first becomes eligible for benefits at age 62 to determine the PIA. Individuals retiring at age 65 receive the full dollar amount of their inflation-adjusted PIA each month. Those retiring before age 65 receive a permanent reduction of the inflation-adjusted PIA benefits of 0.56 percent per month of early retirement. A person retiring at age 62 will receive 80 percent of his or her PIA per month. When normal retirement age increases in the future, the percentage reduction for early retirement will increase. People retiring after age 65 receive a permanent percentage increase in the cost-of-living-adjusted PIA. The increase in PIA for people attaining age 62 in 1998 is 6 percent per year of postponed retirement past the normal retirement age, and it is scheduled to rise to 8 percent per year in the year of 2009.

After a person begins receiving benefits, the Social Security Administration adjusts them each year to reflect changes in cost of living. It normally determines the cost of living adjustment through use of the Consumer Price Index for Urban Wage Earners and Clerical Workers. When a trust fund's resources at the beginning of the year fall below 20 percent of the estimated outgo for the following 12 months, a financial stabilizer provision becomes applicable. Under these conditions the Social Security Administration uses either the Consumer Price Index or the average wage increase, whichever is lower, to set cost of living adjustments. These adjustments may not produce an increase in some years, but they are not permitted to reduce prior benefits.

Family Benefits

Eligibility

Families of retired and disabled Social Security beneficiaries receive family benefits based on the worker's earnings record subject to certain eligibility requirements. Spouses must have been married to the worker for least one year and be 62 years of age or older to receive retirement benefits. A spouse of a retired or disabled worker is eligible to receive benefits at any age if she or he is caring for the worker's entitled children who are less than 16 years of age. He or she is also eligible if caring for an entitled disabled child 18 years of age or older who was disabled before age 22.

Some currently unmarried divorced spouses of a retired or nonretired worker are eligible to receive retirement benefits based on the work record of the former spouse. The marriage must have lasted at least 10 years for a divorced spouse to be eligible. If an unmarried divorced spouse had several former marriages that lasted 10 years or longer, the Social Security administration will use the record of the worker in the former marriage that results in the highest benefits. Both the former spouse and the worker must be 62 years of age or older for a divorced spouse to be eligible.

The Social Security Administration generally follows state laws in determining marital status. Marriages that are legal under state law are recognized as valid. Common-law marriages are recognized if they took place in states where they are legal. Same-sex marriages are not recognized. The federal Defense of Marriage Act of 1996 prohibits the Social Security program from recognizing same-sex marriages even if states decide to recognize them as legal.

A retired or disabled worker's unmarried children who are less than 18 years of age are eligible to receive monthly benefits. Unmarried children less than 19 years of age are eligible for these benefits if they are full-time elementary or high school students. To be eligible the worker's child must be legitimate; illegitimate, but acknowledged in writing to be the worker's child; legally adopted; or a stepchild. Stepchildren must receive at least one-half of their support from the worker in order to be an eligible dependent. Children less than 18 years of age who are supported by and are living with their grandparents may be eligible for benefits based on their grandparent's earnings record. In such cases the children's parents must be dead or totally disabled.

Spouses, divorced spouses, and children are subject to the earnings test. If they have earnings beyond a specified maximum, they will lose some or all of their benefits. The Social Security Administration determines this deduction in the same way that it does for retirees.

Benefits

When the spouse of a retired or disabled worker begins drawing retirement benefits at age 65 based on the worker's contributions, she or he will receive 50 percent of the retired worker's full, age 65, PIA. The spouse will receive a reduction in the benefit amount for each month before age 65 that benefits begin. Spousal retirement benefits at age 62 are 37.5 percent of the retired or disabled worker's full benefit amount. When the normal retirement age increases to be greater than 65 in the future, the percentage of PIA received in spousal benefits for a person of a given age will be adjusted downward. Spousal benefits may sometimes be altered by the receipt of governmental pensions from work not covered by Social Security.

Spousal benefits for individuals caring for entitled children are 50 percent of the retired or disabled worker's full benefit amount or PIA. Eligible unmarried children of a retired or disabled worker receive 50 percent of the worker's full benefit amount.

Some individuals are eligible for retirement benefits based on their own work records and on their spouse's work record. In such cases the benefit will be the amount provided for by their own work record if that amount is greater than the amount that they would receive in spousal benefits. If the benefit amount they would receive in spousal benefits is greater, they will receive the benefits based on their own record plus a supplemental amount to bring them up to the level of the spousal benefit.

Family benefits are limited to a maximum amount. The worker's benefits and benefits paid to a former spouse are not included in this family maximum. Family maximums range between 150 and 188 percent of a worker's PIA. If children are eligible for benefits based on the work history of both parents, the family maximum is higher than the maximum for either parent (Landis 1993, p. 55).

Disability Benefits

Eligibility

The Social Security program requires the certification of a person's substantial and long-lasting disability in order for him or her to qualify for disability benefits. A person must be unable to engage in any substantial gainful activity due to a physical or mental impairment. Substantial gainful activity for people who are not blind is the ability to earn wages of $500 per month after subtracting impairment-related work expenses. For blind persons it is the ability to earn $1,050 per month after subtracting impairment-related work expenses. After 1996 applicants' drug addiction and/or alcoholism excludes them from eligibility if the condition contributes materially to their impairment (Social Security Administration 1998, p. 40).

The medical condition must be expected to last continuously for at least twelve months or to result in death. The program bases evidence for eligibility on reports of a person's medical condition, medical records, and vocational and educational background. The Social Security Administration contracts with state governments to decide the medical eligibility of applicants for disability insurance. In most states the determination of the person's medical eligibility for disability benefits is made by the State Department of Health.

To be eligible for Social Security disability benefits a person must have both substantial lifetime work and recent work. The requirements to meet these standards vary according to a person's age. People who are between 31 and 42 years of age when they become disabled must have 20 quarters of credit in covered employment within the last 10 years. People who are older than 42 years of age at the time of disablement must have one additional quarter of credit within the last 10 years for each year of age increase. Those who are less than 31 years of age must have credits for one-half of the quarters between their twenty-first birthday and the time of their disability.

Dependent spouses or former spouses are eligible for retirement benefits, subject to retirement rules, based on the disabled worker's earnings record. Dependent spouses are also eligible for benefits if they are caring for the disabled worker's dependent children, as specified in the rules for family benefits. The disabled worker's dependent children are eligible for cash benefits as determined by family benefit rules.

A disabled widow or widower may be eligible for disability benefits based on the work record of his or her deceased spouse. A disabled surviving divorced spouse may be eligible for disability benefits based on the work record of his or her deceased former spouse. Disabled widows, widowers, or surviving divorced spouses would benefit from using the eligibility based on the former spouse's work record when the benefits would be greater than those generated by using their own work record. They would also benefit when they are not eligible to use their own work record.

To receive disability benefits on a former spouse's record the disabled widow or widower must be currently unmarried or have remarried after the age of 60. A disabled surviving divorced spouse must have been married to the deceased worker for at least 10 years and be currently unmarried or have remarried after the age of 60. In addition the recipient must be at least 50 years of age and be certified to have a substantial and long-lasting disability based on the same criteria that are applicable to other disabled individuals. The disability must have begun before the worker's death or within a period of seven years after the worker's death. Alternatively, for those who were previously eligible for Social Security benefits because they were caring for the deceased worker's children, the disability must have started before those payments ended or within seven years after they ended. This alternative allows a later occurrence of disability for people who received survivors benefits because they were caring for a deceased worker's children.

Disabled adult children of a worker who is retired, disabled, or deceased are eligible for Social Security disability benefits under certain conditions. They must be unmarried. The adult child's disability must have begun before he or she was 22 years of age. The physical or mental impairment must meet the same qualifications as that of a disabled worker.

Benefits

Monthly cash payments are made to individuals certified as disabled. Average monthly payments are at approximately the same level that a person would receive when retiring at age 65. Benefits for retired spouses of disabled workers and spouses caring for a disabled worker's dependent children are as noted in the section on family benefits. Benefit payments to a disabled widow, widower, or surviving divorced spouse are at the level of 71.5 percent of the worker's full benefit amount or PIA. Eligible disabled adult children receive 50 percent of a living parent's full benefits and 75 percent of the deceased parent's full benefits.

A person certified to be disabled begins to be credited with cash benefits on the first day of the month that follows a five-full-month wait after the onset of the disability. The actual first payment is sent at the beginning of the following month. If more than five months have elapsed between the time of becoming disabled and certification of eligibility for benefits, the disabled person and family may receive back payments for up to twelve months before the month of filing for benefits.

Social Security payments may be reduced for recipients of pensions or disability payments derived from governmental employment not covered under the Social Security system. For example, people may not receive more than 80 percent of their average predisability earnings from the combined sources of workers' compensation and Social Security disability benefits. Either Social Security disability benefits or workers' compensation benefits, or both, will be reduced to meet this requirement.

After a person has been entitled to disability benefits for 24 months, he or she becomes eligible for Medicare benefits. The 24-month period starts on the month that a person's cash benefits begin. The Medicare benefits are the same as those provided for retirees who are 65 years old.

The Social Security disability program provides work incentives to promote a recipient's return to employment. Those returning to work may do so with no monetary penalty for nine consecutive or non-consecutive months in which they receive $200 or more in wages or have 40 or more self-employed work hours. Earnings of less than $200 per month do not count as a part of the trial work period. When a person shows an ability to earn $500 per month or more continually, disability checks will be stopped after a grace period of three months. After the disability checks stop, the program provides an extended period of eligibility for 36 consecutive months. During this period a person's disability benefit will be paid when his or her earnings fall below the substantial work limit of $500 per month. Medicare coverage continues during this 36-month period regardless of earnings level. When Medicare coverage stops, the program provides an option to purchase that coverage by paying a monthly premium.

Survivors Benefits

Eligibility

Widows and widowers of fully insured workers are eligible for survivors benefits under specified conditions. They must be 60 years of age or older. They must be currently unmarried or have remarried after age 60 years to qualify. To be fully insured the worker must have had 40 work credits if he or she died at age 62 or older. Regulations provide a fully insured status for individuals with one less work credit per year of earlier death. If a person died at age 28 or younger, he or she must have had six work credits to be fully insured. Surviving divorced spouses of a marriage that lasted 10 years or longer are also eligible for benefits. Their eligibility is based on their former spouse's contributions under the same criteria that applies to widows or widowers.

Unmarried children of an insured worker who are less than 18 years of age, or less than 19 years of age if they are attending elementary or high school full-time, are eligible for survivors benefits. In either instance, the deceased parent must have been either fully or currently insured. A parent would have been currently insured if they worked one and one-half years or more during the three years before their death.

Widows, widowers, and surviving divorced spouses under age 60 are eligible to receive survivors benefits if they are caring for the worker's child who is less than 16 years of age. They are also eligible if caring for an entitled disabled child, 18 years of age or older, who is receiving benefits based on the deceased worker's earnings record. In order for them to be eligible the deceased worker must have been either fully or currently insured.

Surviving dependent parents who are age 62 or over are eligible for survivors benefits. Natural parents, stepparents, and adoptive parents may also be qualified. To be considered dependent the parent must have received one-half or more of their support from the worker before his or her death. The deceased worker must have been fully insured in order for the dependent parents to be eligible.

Benefits

Surviving widows, widowers, and divorced spouses who begin drawing benefits at age 65 or later are eligible to receive 100 percent of the deceased worker's full PIA plus any delayed retirement credit the deceased worker would be receiving. When a worker dies before receiving Social Security retirement checks, the survivor receives 100 percent of the worker's full, age 65, benefit amount or PIA. The Social Security Administration reduces the surviving spouse's benefits if the deceased worker received Social Security before the normal retirement age and the surviving spouse first became entitled to benefits at age 62 or later. Under those circumstances, the administration limits the surviving spouse's benefit at age 65 to the amount the worker would be receiving if still living or 82.5 percent of the worker's PIA, whichever is greater.

Surviving windows, widowers, divorced spouses, and children who do not pass the retirement test because of earnings beyond a specified maximum will lose some or all of their benefits. The Social Security Administration determines this deduction in the same way that it does for retirees.

Survivors who begin receiving benefits before age 65 will have permanently reduced benefits. They receive a 0.475 percent per month reduction for each month of earlier receipt. Survivors who begin benefits at age 60 get 71.5 percent of the worker's benefits. The age to receive full survivors benefits will gradually increase beginning in the year 2005. By the year 2029 the full benefit age will be 67 years. The amount payable at age 60 will remain at 71.5 percent of the worker's benefits, but the percent reduction per month will be adjusted. Social Security recipients who have governmental pensions from work not covered in the Social Security system may receive reduced benefits.

Eligible children receive benefits equal to 75 percent of the deceased parent's full benefit amount or PIA. Eligible widows, widowers, and surviving divorced spouses less than 60 years of age who care for a worker's children receive amounts equal to 75 percent of the deceased worker's PIA. Each eligible dependent parent gets 75 percent of the deceased worker's full benefit amount when there are two eligible parents. If there is only one eligible parent, she or he receives 82.5 percent of the deceased worker's PIA. Social Security rules specify a family maximum payment that places limits on the amount of benefits payable to large families.

Social Security may pay a lump-sum death benefit to the survivors of a worker who was fully or currently insured. This payment is paid to the surviving spouse if she or he lived with the worker at the time of death. Surviving spouses not living with the worker at that time will receive the lump-sum payment if they were eligible for survivors benefits on the worker's record during the month of death. Former spouses are not eligible for lump-sum death benefits. In cases without an eligible spouse, the benefit may be paid to the deceased worker's children if they were eligible for survivors benefits on the worker's record in the month of death. Lump-sum death benefits cannot be paid directly to a funeral home. An applicant for these benefits must apply within two years of the worker's death.

Medicare Benefits

The Medicare program pays covered medical expenses for people who are 65 or over, disabled, or who have chronic kidney disease. It pays only for services given in the United States with a few exceptions. The Part A program or Hospital Insurance (HI) provides coverage for the costs of hospital care. The Part B program or Supplemental Medical Insurance (SMI) covers medical bills outside the hospital. The Medicare+Choice program allows people to elect to receive services through managed care organizations rather than through a fee-for-service arrangement. Medicare+Choice is Part C of Medicare.

Medicare offers people who enroll in Part B insurance a six-month open enrollment period in Medigap insurance during which they cannot be refused due to a pre-existing medical condition. Medigap insurance is private insurance that supplements Medicare coverage. Individuals purchase Part B and Medigap insurance at their option. General revenue taxes supplement the costs of Part B insurance, making it more valuable than the premiums charged for it. Most people eligible for enrollment should purchase Part B insurance. They also need Medigap insurance to provide important health services not covered by Medicare (Rejda 1999, p. 234).

Eligibility

People 65 years of age or over are eligible to receive Part A and Part B benefits. Those eligible for Social Security retirement benefits or Railroad Retirement Board benefits are not charged additional premiums for Part A benefits. Federal employees not covered by Social Security also receive Part A benefits without additional cost. Aged persons not having sufficient work credits to be eligible for Social Security benefits may elect to pay a premium for Part A coverage. Anyone 65 years of age or older can purchase Part B coverage by paying a monthly premium.

Disabled people under age 65 can receive Part A and Part B after being eligible to receive Social Security disability benefits for at least 24 continuous or noncontinuous months. The program provides insurance for disabled workers, a covered worker's disabled widow or widower age 50 and older, and a covered worker's disabled children 18 years of age or older who became disabled before age 22. Eligible disabled persons do not pay for Part A insurance. They may voluntarily elect to receive Part B benefits by paying a monthly premium.

People with an end-stage renal disease of any age are eligible for Part A and Part B benefits if they are fully or currently insured. They must wait for three months after beginning treatment for the renal condition to begin receiving benefits. Family members of the covered worker are eligible only if they also have end-stage renal disease. Eligible persons with an end-stage renal disease do not pay for Part A. They may elect to pay a monthly premium for Part B.

Application Process

Those eligible must enroll in Medicare to receive benefits. People who are retired and drawing Social Security before they reach the age of 65 will be automatically enrolled in both Part A and Part B. They may elect to drop enrollment in Part B. Those not automatically enrolled need to apply for Part A and, optionally, for Part B insurance. They should apply during an initial enrollment period unless they have continuing coverage under an employer's health insurance plan. The initial enrollment period begins three months before their sixty-fifth birthday and lasts for seven months. To begin Medicare coverage at age 65 the application must be made during the first three months of the initial enrollment period. Persons applying during the last four months of the initial enrollment period must wait one to three months after enrollment for coverage to begin.

Workers and their spouses with continuing coverage under an employer's health insurance plan may delay enrolling for Medicare until coverage from work ends. They would then enroll during a "special enrollment period." This period allows enrollment any time while covered by the employer's health insurance plan or in the eight-month period after employment ends or health coverage ends, whichever comes first. Persons enrolling during the month of termination of employment, or termination of health insurance, receive Medicare coverage on the first day of the enrollment month. Those who enroll after the month of termination of employment, or termination of health insurance, will begin to receive Medicare coverage in the month after they enroll.

Persons with an employer's health insurance plan may decide to delay Medicare coverage. Medicare will be a secondary payer that pays only for expenses not covered under the employer's plan. Immediate enrollment in Part A will be advantageous for most persons since it is provided without additional premiums. Delay of enrollment in Part B, however, may be advantageous. In some cases Part B will provide few or no benefits beyond those of the employer's plan.

When people first enroll in Part B of Medicare, they have a nonrepeatable six-month period with guaranteed enrollment in a Medigap health insurance policy with no refusal due to poor health. This opportunity will be forfeited if they do not enroll in a Medigap policy during the six-month period. This provides an additional reason to delay enrollment in Part B coverage when covered under an adequate employer's health insurance plan. However, it is important to evaluate carefully the adequacy of the medical and health-related services provided in the employer's plan before deciding not to purchase Part B Medicare and Medigap coverage.

A general enrollment period is available for those who apply after the initial or special enrollment period. The general enrollment period is from January 1 to March 31 of each year. Coverage begins July 1 of the year that a person enrolls. The premiums for Part B coverage are permanently increased by 10 percent for each year of delay in enrollment.

Part A Benefits

Part A of Medicare coverage pays for part of inpatient hospital care, care in a skilled nursing home, home health services benefits, and hospice care. Medicare pays the entire bill for the first 60 days of inpatient hospital care except for a deductible. A deductible must be paid in each benefit period, which begins upon entry to a hospital and ends 60 days after discharge. Medicare recipients hospitalized more than 60 consecutive days pay approximately $200 per day for days 61 through 90. Stays in the hospital beyond 90 consecutive days require that the patient pay all charges or elect to use some or all of their 60 nonrenewable lifetime reserve days, costing approximately $400 per day. The deductible amount and the daily care charges for stays beyond 60 days are increased each year to adjust for inflation.

Part A provides hospital coverage for a semiprivate room, nursing care, medications, meals, operating and recovery room costs, anesthesia services, rehabilitation services, lab tests, X rays, and other supplies and services. It does not cover doctors' services, private rooms, private nurses, or convenience items such as telephones and television sets. Hospital Insurance covers up to 190 days of inpatient treatment in a psychiatric hospital. This coverage is provided only once in a lifetime and cannot be renewed.

Medicare reimburses hospitals under a prospective payment system (PPS). Payments are determined in advance using a classification system of over 500 diagnostic related groups (DRG). Hospitals receive a single payment amount for care given to a person with a specific classified diagnosis. The program identifies 495 diagnostic related groups. A reimbursement paid to a hospital varies in relation to the facility's urban or rural location. It normally does not vary according to the medical needs of a person with a given diagnosis. Hospitals must absorb costs that exceed the flat DRG amount, but they gain financial benefits when treatment costs are less than the flat DRG amount. The system promotes operating efficiency but limits the physician's ability to make treatment decisions. It gives a monetary incentive to shorten hospital stays despite individual medical needs (Rejda 1999, p. 225).

Part A insurance pays for all covered charges for the first 20 days of skilled nursing care. For days 21 through 100 Medicare Part A pays for all covered services beyond a deductible amount of approximately $100 per day. It does not pay for skilled nursing home services beyond 100 days in a given benefit period. A benefit period for skilled nursing home services ends 60 days after a person's discharge. The Social Security Administration uses a prospective payment system to reimburse skilled nursing homes.

Services covered include a semiprivate room, meals, rehabilitation services, nursing services, medications, medical supplies, and appliances. Medicare provides coverage only when services are given in a skilled nursing facility following a person's hospital stay of at least three days. It does not cover custodial nursing home care.

Part A insurance provides home health care benefits following a person's hospital stay of at least three days or a stay in a skilled nursing facility. It covers homebound persons who need physical therapy, speech therapy, or skilled nursing care on a part-time or intermittent basis. Part A covers the entire range of home health care services for persons enrolled in Part A but not Part B. For persons enrolled in both Part A and Part B, the first 100 postinstitutional visits per year are covered by Part A. Part B covers the first 100 non-postinstitutional home care visits. Part A coverage of home health care for non-postinstitutional visits will be phased out in the future. The Social Security Administration uses a prospective payment system to reimburse home health care providers.

Medicare pays for the entire cost of covered home health services. The insurance provides 28 hours per week or less of home health care for up to 21 consecutive days to individuals who are confined at home. It pays for 80 percent of the expenses for durable medical equipment. Covered home health benefits include medical social services, physical therapy, speech therapy, services from home health aides, occupational therapy, intermittent or part-time skilled nursing care, and certain medical supplies and equipment. Full-time nursing care at home, meals, homemaker services, blood, and medications are not covered.

Part A insurance covers hospice care for terminally ill people with a life expectancy of 6 months or less. Part A of Medicare pays for two 90-day periods. Physicians can authorize coverage for additional 60-day periods of hospice care by certifying that the beneficiary continues to be terminally ill. Hospices are reimbursed at one of four predetermined rates related to the level of care provided.

Covered hospice services include doctor's care, nursing care, medical social services, counseling, physical therapy, speech therapy, occupational therapy, services from a home health aide, and homemaker services. Most services are provided at home, but short-term inpatient care is covered. Medications are covered except for a 5 percent deductible. Covered services must be provided by a Medicare-certified hospice.

Part B Benefits

Supplementary Medical Insurance or Part B of Medicare pays for physicians' services received in the doctor's office, the hospital, or elsewhere. It pays for outpatient hospital care, diagnostic tests, X-ray and other radiation therapy, physical and speech therapy, home dialysis supplies and equipment, rural health clinic services, durable medical equipment, and ambulance services. Part B pays the costs of covered non-postinstitutionalized home health services for homebound individuals for up to 100 visits per year. SMI covers mammograms for women over the age of 40, periodic pap smears, and colorectal screening. The program extensively limits services from chiropractors, podiatrists, dentists, and optometrists. Medicare pays physicians on a fee-for-service basis that is updated each year.

Supplemental Medical Insurance does not cover routine dental and vision care. It does not cover preventive measures such as physical examinations and cholesterol testing. The program does not cover most expenses for prescriptions. It does not cover long-term care in a nursing home or full-time nursing care at home.

People enrolled in Supplementary Medical Insurance pay a monthly premium plus an annual deductible of $100 per year. Medicare pays 80 percent of allowable charges beyond the deductible. Charges higher than an allowable amount set by Medicare must be paid for by the patient. Medicare requires that doctors file payment claims directly with them rather than billing the patient. Doctors cannot charge more than 115 percent of the Medicare allowed charge. This cap limits the costs that can be passed on to the patient and may help in combating rising health care costs.

Managed Care

Persons receiving Medicare services may elect to obtain them through the traditional fee-for-service system or through a managed care organization that has a payment agreement with Medicare. Prior to 1998, service from managed care organizations was authorized by the Tax Equity and Fiscal Responsibility Act of 1982, which established the Medicare Risk Contract Program. The Balanced budget act of 1997 replaced the risk program, beginning in 1998, with a program called Medicare+Choice.

Medicare+Choice provides more plan options and makes payments under a new capitation system. All plans except Medical Savings Accounts must cover all benefits provided under the current Medicare benefit package. This program is Part C of Medicare. Almost all individuals covered by Medicare Part A and B have an option to receive benefits either through the fee-for-service arrangement or the Medicare+Choice program. Initially beneficiaries are entitled to enroll at any time in a Medicare+Choice program that serves their area. Plans may exclude individuals from coverage who qualify for Medicare on the basis of end-stage renal disease. Plans may also deny enrollment if they have reached the limits of their enrollment capacity. Beginning in 2002 persons can change plan options only during an annual election period.

Insurance to Supplement Medicare

To cover some medical services not provided by Part A or Part B of Medicare many individuals purchase Medigap insurance. Private insurance companies develop these policies to provide selected services not covered by Medicare. They offer these policies in 10 standardized types. The policies have various levels and types of coverage at a variety of prices.

Some managed care organizations provide services similar to those provided through Medigap insurance. These plans may or may not charge an additional premium for the expanded coverage. Costs vary with the scope of expanded coverage (Landis 1993, p. 133).

Medicare and Medigap plans do not cover the costs of long-term medical care. Coverage for the costs of long-term care in nursing homes, adult family homes, assisted living, and adult daycare must be covered by private means or by welfare programs. A variety of private insurance policies to cover these costs are available and need to be evaluated by individuals as a part of their plans for meeting health care costs.

References

Landis, A. 1993. *Social Security: The Inside Story*. Bellevue, WA: Mount Vernon Press.

Rejda, G. E. 1999. *Social Insurance and Economic Security*. (6th ed.). Englewood Cliffs, NJ: Prentice Hall.

Social Security Administration 1998. Annual Statistical Supplement Updates for 1998. *Social Security Bulletin, 61*(2).

Steuerle, C. E., & Bakija, J. M. 1994. *Retooling Social Security for the 21st Century: Right and Wrong Approaches to Reform.* Washington, DC: Urban Institute Press; distributed by National Book Network.

Chapter 3

Finance

Due to budget reduction measures, the light at the end of the tunnel
has been turned off until further notice.
—Flier posted in the bill room at Colorado Legislature

Social Security Taxes

Payroll taxes are the primary source of revenue for Social Security programs. In 1998 payroll taxes provided approximately 86 percent of the total income received by the Old Age and Survivors Insurance (OASI) trust fund and 91 percent for the DI trust fund. The Federal Insurance Contributions Act imposes Social Security taxes on salaried workers. The Self-Employment Contributions Act (SECA) requires those who are self-employed to pay Social Security taxes. Workers currently pay 7.65 percent of their salaries up to a maximum salary level in Social Security taxes. Employers match the tax paid by each worker, resulting in a total FICA tax rate of 15.3 percent of the worker's salary (Executive Office of the President, Office of Management and Budget 1998b, pp. 1004–1006).

The Old Age, Survivors, and Disability Insurance (OASDI) program receives revenues from FICA taxes equal to 12.4 percent of the workers' salaries, with 10.6 percent distributed to OASI and 1.8 percent distributed to DI. Workers paid OASDI taxes on earnings up to $68,400 in 1998. The maximum salary on which taxes are paid increases each year in correspondence to increases in average wages in the economy.

People who are self-employed pay 12.4 percent of their adjusted net earnings up to a maximum earnings level as taxes for the OASDI programs. They adjust their net earnings by deducting 7.65 percent of them before computing Social Security taxes. Adjusted net earnings equal 92.35 percent of total net earnings. Self-employed people pay OASDI taxes on the same maximum of

38

adjusted net earnings as do employees on their salaries. They are allowed to deduct one-half of their Social Security taxes as a business expense for income tax purposes.

Hospital insurance payroll taxes are the primary source of funding for Part A of Medicare. The Hospital Insurance program receives revenues from FICA taxes equal to 2.9 percent of a worker's salary. The self-employed pay 2.9 percent of their adjusted net earnings as taxes for the HI program. They pay taxes for HI on all adjusted net earnings without a limit. The HI trust fund also receives revenues from the taxation of OASDI benefits as provided by the 1993 income tax provisions.

Premiums paid by beneficiaries finance approximately 25 percent of Medicare Part B expenses. Federal general revenues finance the balance of these expenses.

Social Security beneficiaries pay taxes on their Social Security benefits when total income is above specified limits. In 1998 approximately $7 billion was collected from individual income taxes on OASI benefits and $436 million on DI benefits. Revenues from taxes on OASDI benefits represent approximately 2 percent of the total income received by the OASI trust fund and less than 1 percent of total DI trust fund income (Landis 1993, p. 236; Executive Office of the President, Office of Management and Budget 1998b, pp.1004–1006).

Trust Funds

Private sector trusts and governmental trusts have different functions and legal mandates. In the private sector the trustee must use the assets of the trust to serve its beneficiaries. Trustees of a private trust cannot unilaterally change the conditions of the trust. Federal trust funds must use their assets for the purposes designated by law. The government can change the purpose for which it uses a trust fund's assets by changing the law (Executive Office of the President, Office of Management and Budget 1998b, pp.1004–1006).

The government deposits Social Security taxes in accounts that it maintains with financial institutions across the country. They become a part of the operating cash pool of the U.S. Treasury. The Treasury issues securities in the form of short-term treasury notes to the Social Security trust funds to account for the taxes received.

Each June the Treasury reinvests the short-term notes that are not needed to pay immediate benefits in long-term Treasury bonds. These federal securities can be either public issues that are available to the public on the open market or special public debt obligations issued exclusively for the trust funds. Most of the federal securities issued to the Social Security trusts in the past were special public debt obligations. The trust funds do not hold money. Benefits are not paid from the trust funds. Benefits are paid by the U.S. Treasury. As Social Security checks are paid, the U.S. Treasury reduces the securities in the trust funds' accounts by an equivalent amount.

The Social Security Act specifies that revenues can only be invested in treasury securities such as notes, bills, and bonds. Securities in the Social Security trust funds earn an interest that is equal to the prevailing average rate on outstanding federal securities with a maturity of four years or longer. Historically these investments have yielded an average real interest rate of 2.7 percent after subtracting inflationary factors. The trust funds receive interest payments as additional treasury securities. In 1998 the trust fund's Treasury securities yielded approximately $41 billion for OASI and $4 billion for DI. This amount represents approximately 10 percent of the total income received by the OASI trust fund and 7 percent of the total income received by the DI trust fund (Executive Office of the President, Office of Management and Budget 1998b, pp.1004–1006).

When the government receives more Social Security taxes than are spent for Social Security programs, they normally use the revenues to finance other operations. The government borrows these funds from the Social Security trust funds. When the government issues federal securities for borrowed funds, it increases the trust fund's balance and adds to the federal deficit (Executive Office of the President, Office of Management and Budget 1998a, pp. 298–299).

Federal securities issued to the Social Security trust funds represent the promise of the U.S. government to pay Social Security benefits when needed in the future. They represent an IOU from one government account to another. The government does not accumulate assets through this process. It spends incoming assets with a promise to replace them at some future date. Securities in the trust funds authorize and obligate the U.S. Treasury Department to use incoming funds to pay current and future Social Security benefits.

Until the 1980s the Social Security trust funds operated on a pay-as-you-go principle also known as current-cost financing. The government set revenue levels to balance expenditures while maintaining a small contingency fund. Workers paid Social Security taxes that financed the payments to current program beneficiaries in this pay-as-you-go system. The Social Security amendments of 1983 increased payroll taxes beyond the level necessary to finance current expenditures. This step was taken to partially prefund program expenditures for the "baby boomers." These amendments changed Social Security's financing from a pay-as-you-go system to a partial-reserve financing system. Projections of the Social Security administration show that future Social Security expenditures will be greater than income. This will require that the trust funds spend their current reserves. Projections show a future decline in fund balances and eventual deficits in financing (Executive Office of the President, Office of Management and Budget 1998a, pp. 299–300).

Budget Issues

In 1969 President Johnson began counting trust fund operations as an official part of the federal budget. This allowed the federal government to have a unified budget that reflected all of the taxes collected and all of the governmental outlays. In the 1970s the federal budget ran large deficits. Politicians searched for ways to cut the budget deficits and as a part of that search they considered cuts in the Social Security programs. To avoid cuts in the Social Security program due to budgetary considerations, legislators passed a series of measures to prevent them. They enacted legislation in 1983, 1985, and 1987 that made the Social Security program a more distinct part of the budget. These acts also permitted legislators to raise congressional floor objections (points of order) to obstruct passage of budget bills containing Social Security changes that would erode the balances of the Social Security trust funds (Warren 1995).

Social Security income substantially exceeded expenditures in the 1980s. In a unified budget these surpluses masked the size of the federal budget deficits. Congress excluded Social Security income and expenditures from all calculations of the federal budget in 1990. This legislation excluded the Social Security program from the budget prepared by the president, from the federal budgets developed by the Congress, and from budget processes designed to reduce and control budget deficits (Warren 1995).

An exception was made for Social Security's administrative expenses. They can be considered as a part of the federal budget process. Congress sets the budgeted amount of expenditures for administration each year. Administrative expenditures are paid for by Social Security trust fund revenues. Typically administrative costs are less than 1 percent of program benefits.

Spending on Social Security represents approximately 19 percent of total federal spending. Social Security receipts represent approximately 27 percent of federal income. A budget that excludes these receipts and expenditures gives only a partial picture of federal operations and their impact on individuals and the economy. Federal budget makers normally prepare a unified budget that specifies on-budget federal fund items and off-budget items such as those for the Social Security programs. The unified budget gives a complete picture of federal expenditures and revenues (Warren 1995).

Since the 1960s, governmental trust funds have paid out increasing amounts of total benefits. Benefits were 4.1 percent of gross domestic product (GDP) in the 1960s. They rose to 8.7 percent of GDP in the 1990s. These figures include all trust funds, with the Social Security trust funds playing a primary role and reflecting this trend. During the same period other federal fund payments remained stable, representing between 14 and 15 percent of GDP. Total spending for this period increased from 19 percent to 23 percent of GDP (Executive Office of the President, Office of Management and Budget 1998a, pp. 298–301).

Since 1960, the government has increased trust fund taxes in relationship to GDP. Overall trust fund receipts were 3.7 percent of GDP in the 1960s. They rose to 7.3 percent of GDP in the 1990s. However, these increases were offset by decreases in federal fund receipts. The government reduced other taxes from 14 to 15 percent of GDP to 10 to 11 percent of GDP. Total budget receipts have remained constant at 18 to 19 percent of GDP since the 1960s. The gap between expenditure levels and tax receipts produces a continually rising federal deficit. The government finances the deficit through federal securities issued to the public and to the Social Security trust funds. If surpluses in these trust funds did not exist, the entire federal deficit would have to be financed through federal securities issued to the public.

In 1998, the government cut total unified budget federal spending to below 20 percent of GDP. Taxes received in 1998 equaled approximately 21 percent of GDP. The Office of Management and Budget projected unified budget surpluses between the years 1999 and 2010. However, when surpluses in the Social Security trust funds and other off-budget surpluses were disregarded, the federal fund balance had a projected deficit of approximately $96 billion in 1999 and had continuing projected deficits for the next few years.

Current surpluses in Social Security taxes are not the means through which the future costs of the system will be met. When the Social Security trust funds draw on the surpluses credited to them, the government will pay them with funds gained through taxation or through borrowing. The future costs of the Social Security system may require increased taxes and/or governmental borrowing from the public (Executive Office of the President, Office of Management and Budget 1998a, pp. 298–301; Brimelow 1998, pp. 60–61).

After 2010, when the baby boomers begin to retire, total federal spending will surge. Projections based on the Bipartisan Commission on Entitlements show that federal spending will increase to 29 percent of GDP by 2030. If tax rates remain constant, federal deficit spending after 2010 will rapidly and constantly increase (Brimelow 1998, pp. 60–61).

Demographic Trends

The elderly population in the United States increased from 9 million in 1940 to approximately 34 million in 1995. Census Bureau projections forecast a population of 80 million persons over age 65 by the year 2050. In 1940 the elderly population made up 7 percent of the population. In the 1990s about 12 percent of the population was elderly. By 2050 approximately 20 percent of the population will be elderly. The comparatively large size of the "baby boom" generation born between the years of 1946 through 1964 partially accounts for the increase in the aged population after the year of 2010. The oldest of the baby boomers become eligible for full retirement benefits in 2012 (Ross 1997).

The life expectancy of people in the United States is increasing. Increased life expectancy is a major factor in the growing proportion of the elderly. In 1940 the life expectancy of people at age 65 was 12 years for men and 13 years for women. Life expectancy at age 65 was 15 years for men and 19 years for women in 1995. The Social Security Administration projects that in the year 2040 life expectancy for persons at age 65 will be 17 years for men and 21 years for women. They base these projections on intermediate assumptions about future mortality rates (Ross 1997).

Fertility rates help to explain the increasing proportion of aged persons in the United States. Fertility rates rose from 2.2 children per woman in 1940 to 3.6 children per woman in 1960. Increased fertility rates during that period account for the large size of the baby boom generation when compared with the generations before and after. Currently the fertility rate is approximately two children per woman. Projections of the Social Security Administration show that the fertility rate will be 1.9 children per woman in 2020. The lower fertility rates after 1960 caused the proportion of elderly people in the population to rise (Ross 1997).

A trend toward early retirement increases the proportion of elderly people who receive Social Security benefits. Early retirement also decreases the number of workers who pay Social Security taxes. The average age at which women retire has remained stable over time. However, a higher percentage of men are retiring between the ages of 60 and 64 than in the past. This increases the problem of financing retirement benefits.

Dependency Ratios

The "aged" dependency ratio is the number of adults ages 20–64 divided by the number of adults 65 years and older in the U.S. population. In 1960, the dependency ratio was 5.8 working age adults per elderly person. By 1995, it was 4.7 and it is expected to decline to 2.7 in 2040. Progressively lower dependency ratios equate to lower proportions of working-age people to pay Social Security taxes to support people who are retired.

The Social Security Administration defines the number of people paying Social Security taxes per aged or disabled Social Security recipient as the "Social Security dependency ratio." This ratio was 3.3 in 1995. Projections show that it will be two workers for each beneficiary in 2030 (Ross 1997).

Economic Trends

A healthy economy increases the ability of people of working age to support retirees receiving Social Security. In a healthy economy the unemployment rate is usually low, as was true in the late 1990s. A low unemployment rate increases the number of people working and paying Social Security taxes.

Healthy economies usually produce a high rate of economic growth that results in higher real inflation-adjusted wages. Higher real wages increase the Social Security taxes that workers pay. This gives a stronger base of monetary support for current retirees. If the economy grows only 1 percent per year faster than the trustees of Social Security project that it will, the OASDI program will remain in balance for the next 75 years.

The Social Security system may need future tax increases to ensure its long-term financial balance. Real wage growth increases the ability of workers to absorb such tax increases. When real wage growth is positive over time, the working generation has a larger income base than the generation of current retirees. For example, a Congressional Budget Office study reports that the wealth and real income of the baby boom generation are greater than those of their parents at a similar age. Between 1945 and 1970 the standard of living approximately doubled. However, since 1970 real wage growth has slowed. The ability of workers and the economy to support the Social Security system in the future is interdependent with future trends in economic growth (Ross 1997).

A higher rate of personal and governmental savings would give greater support to growth in the economy. Savings fosters investments that increase productivity and economic growth. Compared with other industrial countries the rate of savings in the United States is currently low. In 1995, the rate of household savings in the United States as a percent of disposable income was 4.7 percent. In 1995, it was 11.6 percent in Germany and 13.4 percent in Japan. In 1999 the personal savings rate in the United States was a minus 1.2 percent (Research and Policy Committee of the Committee for Economic Development 1997, p. 6).

Large federal deficits, which the government covers through borrowing, also divert resources from private investment. Federal deficits lower the national savings rate while budget surpluses increase the national savings rate. Social policies that promote private savings and lessen governmental borrowing combined with constant or decreasing tax rates would support economic growth (Rejda 1999, p. 139).

Financial Soundness

The Social Security trust funds are not fully funded. A trust fund would need to have sufficient accumulated assets to cover all liabilities for accrued benefits at any point in time to be fully funded. Full funding would promote financial soundness for the Social Security trusts. The trusts would not have to rely on future economic growth to provide a satisfactory level of future revenues under conditions of full funding. However, full funding could produce negative economic consequences such as economic deprivation for some people and deflationary pressures that promote high rates of unemployment.

Trusts that provide pension benefits for private plans need full funding to ensure financial soundness. Social Security trust funds can be financially sound without full funding because of an assured basis of future funding. Social Security taxes are compulsory, which gives a basis for continued funding on a pay-as-you-go plan. If financial problems arise, the government has the power to remedy them through taxation or borrowing (Rejda 1999, p. 149–150).

Federal laws require that the Social Security trust funds must have sufficient assets to cover expenditures in order to authorize the payment of benefits. Trustees of the OASI and DI trust funds assert short-term financial adequacy if a trust fund has a sufficient projected reserve balance at the end of the next 10-year period. The projected reserve balance must pay for at least 100 percent of the projected annual expenditures at the end of the next 10-year period for the funds to have short-term financial adequacy (Ways and Means Committee

1998).

Social Security trustees base long-term financial adequacy of the trust funds on the next 75 years of operations. This period is long enough to cover the anticipated retirement years of those currently in the workforce. The trustees determine financial adequacy based on income rates and cost rates expressed as percentages of the projected taxable payroll. Income rates are compared with cost rates over the 75-year period. The trustees adjust estimates of financial adequacy to reflect economic growth or deterioration by basing them on the projected taxable payroll. Most projections assume that the economy will continue to grow over time.

In making future projections the Social Security Administration discounts the costs of future expenditures and the value of future revenues to current dollar values. Discounting determines current dollar values in relation to the time of receipt of revenues and the time that expenditures occur. The sooner revenues of a given amount are received the more valuable they are, and the later expenditures of a given amount occur the less costly they are in current dollar values. Discounting allows the administration to estimate such things as the value of a dollar received today as compared to its value if received 10 years from now. In relation to costs, discounting estimates such things as the cost of an expenditure of a given amount today as compared to its cost if paid 10 years from now.

Income rates and cost rates need to be in near balance over a 75-year period in order for the trustees to conclude that a trust fund has long-term actuarial balance. To be in balance a trust fund must have no projected deviation between income rates and cost rates for at least the next 10 years. The amount of acceptable deviation from the balance between projected income rates and cost rates gradually rises each year after 10 years. By the seventy-fifth year the acceptable projected deviation between income rates and cost rates is 5 percent. A projected deficit of income rates compared to cost rates over the 75-year period by more than the acceptable deviation would show that the Social Security trust funds lack long-term financial adequacy (Ways and Means Committee 1998).

Long-term projections of costs and income of the Social Security program are affected by demographic factors, economic factors, and program benefit levels. The Social Security Administration uses three sets of alternative economic and demographic assumptions when making projections. They use optimistic assumptions, intermediate assumptions, and pessimistic assumptions. Intermediate assumptions are considered to provide the most valid estimate of future solvency. Long-range projections to 75 years in the future are subject to considerable error (Ways and Means Committee 1998).

The OASI trust fund is in excellent financial and health in the short term. This trust fund currently has reserves equal to approximately 200 percent of annual expenditures. Between years of 2010 and 2015 the trust fund has projected reserves of approximately 300 percent of annual expenditures (Ways and Means Committee 1998).

The OASI trust fund does not meet the test for long-term financial adequacy. The Social Security Administration estimates that the trust fund will become exhausted in 2031. It estimates that incoming tax revenues will pay for about three-fourths of the program costs after the fund is depleted in 2031. Income rates are greater than cost rates until 2015. After 2015, cost rates exceed income rates by progressively larger amounts. Using intermediate assumptions the income rate in 2075 will be 11.49 percent of taxable payroll and the cost rate will be 16.85 percent of the taxable payroll (Ways and Means Committee 1998).

The DI trust fund has sufficient reserves to meet the test of short-term financial adequacy. This fund currently has reserves equal to approximately 150 percent of annual expenditures. The fund has projected reserves of at least 100 percent of annual projected expenditures until the year of 2010 when reserves will drop to 95 percent of expenditures. Reserves in the OASI trust fund may at some point in the future be diverted to the DI trust fund to increase its span of financial adequacy. However, currently no legal authority exists for interfund borrowing between OASI and DI (Ways and Means Committee 1998).

The DI trust fund lacks long-term financial adequacy. Estimates of the Social Security Administration project that the fund will become exhausted by 2015. Income rates are greater than cost rates until 2003. After 2003, cost rates exceed income rates by progressively greater amounts. Using intermediate assumptions the income rate in 2075 will be 1.85 of the taxable payroll and the cost rate will be 2.57 of the taxable payroll (Ways and Means Committee 1998).

The Social Security Administration projects that the combined OASDI trust funds will be exhausted in 2029. For the period between 1997 and 2071, it projects an average 2.23 percent of taxable payroll deficit for the combined OASDI program using intermediate assumptions. The program lacks actuarial balance over the next 75 years. Income from OASDI payroll taxes currently is 12.4 percent of the taxable payroll. Income is projected to rise to 13.34 percent of the taxable payroll 75 years from now. OASDI expenditures for benefit payments and administrative expenses are currently 11.49 percent of the taxable payroll. The cost rate will rise to 19.42 percent of the taxable payroll by 2075 under intermediate assumptions.

Trustees of the Hospital Insurance Trust Fund report that the program fails to meet both the short-range and long-range tests of financial adequacy. They estimate that the HI fund will become exhausted by 2010. Cost rates will exceed income rates by progressively increasing amounts after 2007.

Federal general revenues and beneficiary premiums are the source of revenues for the SMI trust fund. The SMI trust fund is of a different type than other Social Security trust funds. Federal general revenues and beneficiary premiums are set each year at a level that will provide solvency. However, the fund faces financial problems because of rising costs. Program costs are expected to rise from 1.7 percent of gross domestic product in 1996 to between four and 5 percent of GDP in 2070. Adequate future funding rests on whether governmental budgetary processes and procedures continue to provide adequate increases.

The nation needs new legislation to resolve the future financial problems of the Social Security system. The longer the delay in dealing with the anticipated future financial problems the more difficult it will be to resolve them. Resolution of the Social Security system's financial problems will require progressively larger future tax increases or benefit cuts as time passes before their implementation. From the perspective of the Social Security system, any current increase in the revenues received compared with benefits paid increases the system's ability to cope with future financial problems. From a national perspective, increases in Social Security revenues received compared with benefits paid will help the nation cope with the future financial burden of paying for Social Security benefits if the surpluses are saved. True savings would occur if the government invests the surpluses or uses them to decrease the national debt owed to the public rather than spending them on other federal programs (Steuerle & Bakija 1994, p. 53–55).

Legislators need to give immediate attention to the provision of financial adequacy for the HI trust fund. This program does not have short-term financial adequacy. The Board of Trustees estimates that the 75-year actuarial deficit for HI is 5.1 percent of projected taxable payroll. Unless costs are contained, the SMI program has projected increases in expenditures that approximately match those of the HI program. Taxpayers will need to pay several more percentage points of their wages in taxes to pay for projected future SMI expenditures. The costs of the public welfare Medicaid program will also rise substantially in the future. The cumulative effects of these increasing medical costs represent a financial problem that is immediate and increasing over time. Legislators need to develop innovative solutions to meet the challenge of providing adequate and cost contained future medical care through these programs (Steuerle & Bakija 1994, p. 53–55).

References

Brimelow, P. 1998. Whose Hand Is That in MY Pocket? *Forbes* (November 30).

Executive Office of the President, Office of Management and Budget. 1998a. *Analytical Perspectives, Budget of the United States Government, Fiscal Year 1998, Other Technical Presentations*. Washington, DC: GPO. Available on the internet at http://www.access.gpo.gov/su_docs/budget98/maindown.html

——. 1998b. *Appendix, Budget of the United States Government, Fiscal Year 1998, Social Security Administration*. Washington, DC: GPO. Available on the internet at http://www.access.gpo.gov /su_docs/budget98/maindown.html

Landis, A. 1993. *Social Security: The Inside Story*. Bellevue, WA: Mount Vernon Press.

Rejda, G. E. 1999. *Social Insurance and Economic Security*. (6th ed.). Englewood Cliffs, NJ: Prentice Hall.

Research and Policy Committee of the Committee for Economic Development. 1997. *Fixing Social Security Executive Summary*. New York: Committee for Economic Development. Available on the internet at http://www.ced.org/docs/ program.htm

Ross, J. L. 1997. *Retirement Income: Implications of Demographic Trends for Social Security and Pension Reform* (HEHS-97-81): GAO Report to the Chairman and Ranking Minority Member, Special Committee on Aging, U.S. Senate.

Steuerle, C. E., & Bakija, J. M. 1994. *Retooling Social Security for the 21st Century: Right and Wrong Approaches to Reform*. Washington, DC: Urban Institute Press; distributed by National Book Network.

Warren, N. 1995. Ask an Actuary, Part VI: Social Security and the Federal Budget. *OASIS Magazine* (September).

Ways and Means Committee. 1998. *1998 Green Book. Section 1. Social Security: The Old-Age, Survivors, and Disability Insurance Programs, Social Security Financing: How the Status of the Trust Funds Is Measured* (DOCID: f: wm007 01.105). Available on the internet at http://aspe.hhs.gov/ 98gb/toc.htm

Chapter 4

Poverty

Where there is no vision, the people perish.
—Proverbs 29:18

Poverty Prevention

Social Security plays a major role in the prevention of poverty in the United States. The OASDHI program reduces the incidence of poverty for aged and disabled individuals and plays a minor but an important role in preventing children's poverty. Both monetary benefits and health benefits help in the prevention of poverty.

The poverty rate among the elderly would be considerably greater without the Social Security program, which taxes working people and transfers the funds to the elderly. The effects of Social Security taxes on working-age poor families may be detrimental in some cases. Some younger families may live at or below poverty levels in part due to Social Security taxes.

The Social Security system taxes poor families at a higher percent of their wages than upper income families. There is an earnings cap set at $68,400, above which individuals do not pay OASDI taxes. There is no earnings cap for taxes on health insurance. The higher tax rate for low-income earners makes OASDI taxes regressive.

The Social Security program computes retirement benefits in a way that is progressive. The basis for computing benefits is a person's Averaged Indexed Monthly Earnings (AIME). The program uses AIME to compute a person's primary insurance amount (PIA). This is the monthly amount of payment that a person would receive if he or she retired at age 65. The benefit formula weights the computed benefits to favor lower income beneficiaries. It allows low-income

51

earners to receive a higher percentage of their former earnings, referred to as a replacement rate, than do high-income earners.

The higher replacement rate for low-income earners helps to avoid high rates of poverty among the elderly population. However, the retirement system has historically had a net regressive effect. People with high incomes have received more funds beyond what they contributed plus a reasonable rate of return than those with low incomes.

Medicare benefits tend to counter the regressive nature of the retirement program. People with low wage earnings have historically received more Medicare benefits beyond the value of their contributions than have high wage earners. The combined effect of retirement and Medicare benefits appear to be slightly progressive for retirees beginning in 2010 in that those with the lowest lifetime incomes receive the largest absolute transfers above what they contributed. Projections for the Social Security system under current rules indicate that this progressivity will increase in the future. (Steuerle & Bakija 1994, p. 106–126).

The federal government issues two different poverty measures. Poverty thresholds are the original federal measure of poverty. Each year the U.S. Census Bureau issues poverty thresholds that it uses for statistical purposes. Each year the department of Health and Human Services issues poverty guidelines. Policy guidelines provide a simplified version of poverty thresholds. The Department of Health and Human Services uses policy guidelines for federal administrative purposes such as determining financial eligibility for federal programs. Numerical values of poverty thresholds and poverty guidelines are quite similar. For example, in 1997 the weighted average poverty threshold for a family of four people was $16,400 while the poverty guideline for a family of four people was $16,050 (U.S. Bureau of the Census 1997c; Department of Health and Human Services 1998, pp. 9235–9238).

The U.S. Census Bureau reports that 13.3 percent of the U.S. population, or 35.6 million people, lived in poverty in 1997. This represents a decline from the poverty rate of 13.7 percent in 1996. The 1997 poverty rate does not show a significant statistical difference from the prerecessionary poverty rate in 1989. A lower percent of persons were poor in 1997 than in the late 1950s, when the poverty rate was 22 percent. Poverty has increased since 1973, when the poverty rate reached a low of 11.1 percent. For people under 18 years of age the poverty rate in 1997 was 19.9 percent. For people 65 years and over the poverty rate was 10.5 percent in 1997 (U.S. Bureau of the Census 1997b).

SOCIAL SECURITY'S PROGRESSIVE BENEFIT FORMULA AND REGRESSIVE

OASDI

In 1996 OASDI benefits provided 40 percent of the aggregate income of aged beneficiaries. The Social Security program classifies persons as aged if they are 65 years of age or over. In 1996 the poverty rate for aged beneficiaries was 9 percent. The poverty rate for these beneficiaries would have been 50 percent without Social Security benefits. Married aged beneficiaries had a poverty rate of 3 percent while unmarried aged beneficiaries had a poverty rate of 16 percent. Without Social Security benefits, the poverty rate would have been 41 percent for aged married beneficiaries and 60 percent for aged unmarried beneficiaries. White aged beneficiaries had a poverty rate of 8 percent while African American aged beneficiaries had a poverty rate of 24 percent. Without Social Security benefits, the poverty rate would have been 49 percent for white aged beneficiaries and 62 percent for African American aged beneficiaries (Apfel 1998, pp. 1–35).

Social Security disability insurance plays an important role in reducing poverty for the disabled. Low-income workers are particularly at risk of impoverishment should they become disabled. This program provided benefits to 26 million disabled people and their families in 1996 at a cost of approximately $43 billion. It has grown considerably since 1957, when it provided benefits for 150,000 disabled workers and their families at a cost of $57 million. The program expanded rapidly during the 1990s. During this period it had a 75 percent increase in the number of beneficiaries and a 125 percent increase in the total amount of benefits. The growth in the program reflects the increased participation of women in the workforce and the growing number of baby boomers who are reaching the age when they are prone to disabilities. It has grown, in part, due to court decisions and changes in laws and regulations that expanded eligibility for benefits (Executive Office of the President, Office of Management and Budget 1998b, pp. 193–196; Burtless 1994, pp. 53–94).

Some individuals receive both OASDI benefits and public assistance benefits through the Supplemental Security Income program (SSI). The proportion of beneficiaries who receive both Social Security and SSI benefits is an indicator of the adequacy of Social Security Benefits. The smaller the proportion the more adequate the Social Security benefits are. SSI extends benefits to aged, blind, and disabled individuals who have inadequate resources that would force them to live near or below poverty levels. In March 1998, 5.5 percent of the 43,941,180 OASDI beneficiaries also received SSI (Social Security Administration 1998, p. 61).

The Social Security program plays a role in reducing poverty for children. Approximately 7.7 million children lived in families that received OASDI and/or SSI benefits in 1996. Of these 7.7 million children, 2.6 million lived in poverty even with the OASDI and/or SSI benefits. Of the remaining 5.1 million children, 1.4 million were kept out of poverty by the OASDI and/or SSI benefits (Apfel 1998, pp. 1–35).

Poverty Gap

The total dollar amount by which the incomes of all poor people fall below the poverty line is termed the poverty gap. In 1995 the poverty gap was $194.5 billion without government benefits. Government benefits provided $135 billion to poor people, which reduced the poverty gap by 69 percent. Poor people received $90 billion from social insurance programs, $43 billion from means-tested programs, and $2 billion from federal tax provisions (Executive Office of the President, Office of Management and Budget 1998a, pp. 189–192).

Social insurance programs are less targeted toward reducing poverty than are means-tested government benefit programs. Only 26 percent of Social Security benefits contributed to the reduction of the poverty gap while 56 percent of means-tested program benefits contributed to its reduction. Although social insurance programs contribute the most to the poverty gap reduction, the means-tested programs are more efficient in reducing poverty. The efficiency of the means-tested programs, however, is reduced by the cost of program administration. Efficiency of these programs is also reduced because some of the funds are used to provide benefits to individuals who are near the poverty line but not impoverished. The Census Bureau data used in determining program efficiency are subject to considerable misreporting of means-tested income (Executive Office of the President, Office of Management and Budget 1998a, pp. pp. 189–192; Burtless 1994, pp. 53–94).

Although Social Security and means-tested income programs play a vital role in reducing poverty, the poverty rates in the United States are comparatively higher than those in other industrialized countries. A study by Burtless compares the poverty rates of Australia, Canada, France, Sweden, the United Kingdom, the United States, and West Germany in the 1980s. The poverty rate of 13.3 percent in the United States was the highest. Canada's 7.0 percent rate was the next highest. West Germany had the lowest overall poverty rate of 2.8 percent. U.S. poverty rates for both children and the elderly were more than double those of any of the other comparable industrialized countries (Burtless 1994, pp. 53–94).

Medical Insurance

Major medical expenses can impoverish individuals and families who would otherwise have sufficient resources to maintain themselves. In the United States 16.1 percent of the population do not have health insurance coverage. Among poor people 31.6 percent are not covered by health insurance, making them vulnerable to even more impoverished conditions. The Medicare program provides health insurance for most people 65 years of age or over. It provides medical insurance for 13.2 percent of all people in the United States and for 13.0

percent of the poor. Medicaid is a public assistance program that provides health benefits for welfare recipients. It provides health benefits for 10.8 percent of all individuals in the United States and for 43.3 percent of the poor. (U.S. Bureau of the Census 1997a).

Medicare insurance provided through the Social Security program significantly reduces poverty due to medical expenses for those 65 years of age or over. Only 1 percent of those individuals do not have health insurance. Of those individuals age 65 or over who are poor only 2.9 percent are without health insurance. However, the Medicare program fails to cover medical services such as long-term care and prescription drugs, leaving some aged persons vulnerable to impoverishment.

Medicare beneficiaries often purchase Medigap insurance to meet some uncovered medical services. Many low-income people are unable to afford this additional coverage. An estimated 15.5 million of the 39 million Medicare recipients do not have Medigap policies. Even middle- and upper-income people may not purchase long-term-care insurance because of such factors as neglect, exclusion due to their morbidity, or its high cost. The lack of this insurance may lead to impoverishment of persons who would otherwise have sufficient income to maintain themselves at or above the poverty line (U.S. Bureau of the Census 1997a).

Steuerle reports that about 20 percent of people 65 years of age or over require long-term-care services. Although family members often provide such care at home, 28 percent of those requiring long periods of care reside in nursing homes. The older a person becomes the more likely it is that he or she will need long-term care. With the average age of the general population growing older, a larger number and percent of population will need such care in the future. The trends toward decreased family sizes and increased participation of women in the labor force may reduce the ability of families to provide lengthy care at home. Impoverishment due to lack of long-term-care insurance seems likely to increase in the future without new public policy initiatives. Medicaid does provide funds for such care, but individuals must be at or near the poverty line to meet the means test for eligibility (Steuerle & Bakija 1994, pp. 142–143).

Wolfe reports a clear association between poor health and poverty. She notes that low-income children are five times more likely to die of cancer, heart disease, and pneumonia/influenza than are children in higher income families. Wolfe summarizes several studies showing that poor health limits earnings. They report a clear relationship between health, labor force participation, and earnings. It seems likely that the lack of medical care for children increases their risk of later impoverishment due to medical problems (Wolfe 1994, pp. 257–259).

Approximately 15 percent of children under than 18 years of age in the United States are not covered by health insurance. The percentage of poor children without health insurance coverage is 23.8. Medicare provides coverage for less than 1 percent of all children and for 1.5 percent of poor children. Medicaid provides medical insurance for 20.5 percent of all children and 60.6 percent of poor children. Children who have health insurance coverage are more likely to receive preventive and primary care than are uninsured children. Insured children with injury, asthma, or an acute earache are more likely to receive treatment than uninsured children with these problems. Uninsured children receive fewer services when admitted to the hospital than do insured children (Executive Office of the President 1998, pp. 89–114).

The Three-Legged Stool

Social Security benefits are targeted toward dual goals. They attempt to provide social adequacy by maintaining standards of living for beneficiaries. They attempt to provide equity by determining benefits to reflect the beneficiary's contributions. Although Social Security is helpful in preventing poverty, the program is not designed to replace adequately the income lost due to disability or retirement. Persons need to have access to other resources to replace the income lost due to retirement or disability.

Cutler discusses the idea of the "three-legged stool" to provide retirement income and prevent poverty. Social Security benefits and other types of social insurance such as Medicare, Workers' Compensation, and Unemployment Insurance represent one leg of the stool. The other two legs are employment-based pensions and individual savings. To provide adequate income and insurance against poverty all three legs supporting the stool need to be strong. If these resources are inadequate, more people will be forced to rely on public assistance programs for subsistence. However, all three legs seem wobbly in the United States. (Cutler 1996, pp. 125–149).

In 1995, heads of households aged 65 or older who lived alone received on average 48 percent of their income from Social Security. They received on average 19 percent of income from employment-related pensions and annuities, 19 percent from dividends and interest, 10 percent from earnings, and 3 percent from public assistance or other federal assistance programs. Their median income was $11,673. Heads of households aged 65 or older living in multiperson families received on average 32 percent of their income from Social Security. They received on average 17 percent of income from employment-related pensions and annuities, 16 percent from dividends and interest, 32 percent from earnings, and 2 percent from public assistance or other federal assistance programs. Their median income was $28,295 (Social Security Administration 1997).

The preceding data show an almost equal contribution to retirement income from employment-related pensions and annuities and from dividends and interest. These sources of income play an important role in preventing poverty. People aged 65 or older living alone received a median of $2,218 per year from each source. Individuals aged 65 or older living in multiperson families received a median of $4,810 per year from employment-related pensions and annuities and $4,527 per year from dividends and interest. Poor people received very little income from either source. Poor individuals aged 65 or older living alone received a median of $167 per year from each source. Individuals aged 65 or older who were poor and living in multiperson families received the median of $342 per year from employment-related pensions and annuities and $205 per year from dividends and interest.

Social Insurance

The Social Security program has income redistributive features that promote poverty reduction. It provides protection against poverty caused by illness and disability. It guards against an inflation-based dissolution of benefits by indexing payments to the cost of living. The Social Security program needs more resources to continue to support people during retirement and disability at current levels. Whether the program can continue to replace income and deter poverty as effectively as it currently does remains in question due to projected declines in trust fund balances and inadequacy of tax revenues (Cutler 1996, pp. 125–149).

Social Security benefits replace up to 90 percent of income reported to Social Security for low-income workers, but only about 30 percent for high-income workers. On average workers receive Social Security benefits equal to 43 percent of preretirement Social Security reported income. Although workers do not necessarily need to replace all employment earnings during retirement to avoid poverty, some need pensions or other savings and resources to remain above the poverty line. Most workers will experience a significant decline in their standard of living if they must rely exclusively on Social Security benefits during retirement (Executive Office of the President, Office of Management and Budget 1998b, pp. pp. 193–196).

Pension Coverage

Employers cover approximately 50 percent of all workers with some form of pension plan. They provide some form of pension plan to 66 percent of workers who are currently nearing retirement age. Employers provide almost 80 percent of unionized workers with retirement plans, but have such plans for only about 40 percent of nonunion workers. Firms with fewer than 20 employees provide these plans for 13 percent of their workers. Large firms with 500 or more employees cover 72 percent of their workers with plans for pensions. Approximately 25 percent of working high school dropouts have pension plans, while approximately 60 percent of employed college graduates have them. Employers provide retirement plans for 27 percent of workers with household incomes of $25,000 or less and for 60 percent of workers with household incomes of $75,000 or more. They provide pension coverage for 51 percent of male workers and 45 percent of female workers. About 49 percent of white workers and 54 percent of African American workers have pension plans (House of Representatives 1996).

The two major types of pensions are defined benefit plans and defined contribution plans. In a defined benefit plan the employer uses a formula to set retirement benefits for individual employees. The formula typically includes such variables as years of service, salary level, and age. An employer is responsible for providing sufficient funds to guarantee payment of the promised benefits. The percentage of employers offering defined benefit plans is declining. In 1993 approximately 9 percent of employers offered only defined benefit plans while 3 percent offered both types of plans.

In a defined contribution plan the employer establishes an individual account for each eligible employee. Most employers contribute a specified percent of the worker's salary to their account. Employees are normally allowed or required to make contributions to their retirement account. Under current laws participants own their contributions and the earnings from them. Employers often establish minimum service requirements that participants must meet before receiving the employer's contributions to the plan. Defined contribution plans are usually more portable than defined benefit plans when employees change jobs. Total funds in an account at the time of retirement determine a person's benefit amount. Employers do not guarantee a level of promised benefits. Employees bear the risk of market forces and economic conditions that affect their retirement funds. The percentage of employers offering defined contribution plans is increasing. In 1992 approximately 87 percent of all pension plans were defined contribution plans.

One type of defined contribution plan is known as a salary reduction plan or as a cash or deferred arrangement (CODA). Various salary reduction plans, or CODAs, are named after the section of the Internal Revenue Code that regulates them. Private for-profit organizations have 401(k) plans. Not-for-profit organizations have 403(b) plans. State and local governments have plans designated as 457 plans. These are salary-reduction plans that allow participants to contribute a nontaxed portion of their salary to a retirement account. Earned income accumulates tax free until an individual withdraws the funds at retirement. Many employers match the worker's contributions to these accounts. Most workers can control, within certain limits, the amount of contributions that they make to the plans. They also normally control the type of investment purchased with account funds within certain limits. In 1992 about 20 percent of all pension plans were 401(k) plans.

Employers who elect to provide pension funds must meet certain minimum legal standards as required by the Employee Retirement Income Security Act of 1974 (ERISA). About $3 trillion in pension assets are safeguarded by the Pension and Welfare Benefits Administration (PWBA). ERISA requires employers to manage funds in the best interest of participants and to inform participants of their rights and obligations. Employers must give adequate disclosure of the plan's terms and activities. ERISA established the Pension Benefit Guaranty Corporation (PBGC) to guarantee the payment of pension benefits in defined benefit plans. The insurance program is financed primarily by employer-paid premiums.

Assets

The average lower income household accumulates very little wealth through private savings or pension funds before retirement. These households accumulate a limited amount of wealth through equity in the home. The average higher income household accumulates a significant amount of financial assets before retirement. In 1989, where the head of a retirement age household had less than a high school education, the median income for the household was $20,100 and the median total wealth was $46,100. For these households the median nonhousing-related wealth was $5,600. Lower income families are most likely to need income beyond Social Security to remain above the poverty level during retirement. Where the head of a retirement-age household had a college degree or higher, the median income was $58,100 and the median total wealth was $210,900. The median nonhousing wealth was $126,000 (Cutler 1996, pp. 125–149).

The following example illustrates the problems faced by low-income workers. Assume that a worker preparing to retire had a current income of $20,100. For purposes of determining Social Security benefits the worker had an Averaged Indexed Yearly Earnings of $18,000 per year and an Average Indexed Monthly Earnings of $1,500. She or he would have a PIA of approximately $757 when calculated with 1998 bend points. The worker would receive Social Security benefits of $757 per month or $9,080 per year if she or he retired at age 65. Poverty guidelines for a one-person family unit specify that a person with an income of $8,050 is living at the poverty line. If the worker had a spouse that received only spousal benefits, the two of them would receive Social Security benefits of $1,135 per month or $13,620 per year. Poverty guidelines for a two-person family unit designate a poverty line of $10,850 per year. In this example Social Security benefits are adequate to maintain the worker living alone or the worker and a spouse at or above the poverty level. However, the Social Security benefits replace only 45 percent of current income for the single worker and only 68 percent of the income of the retired couple.

If total wealth for this household was $46,100, with $5,600 of the total in nonhousing-related wealth, there would not be enough capital to provide a replacement for all of the lost earnings. If the entire $46,100 could be invested at 0.06 percent, it would produce an income of $2,766 per year. The produced income equals approximately 14 percent in of current income. Social Security benefits plus interest from assets would replace 59 percent of the income for a single person and 82 percent for a couple.

Housing wealth is often not liquid and may be difficult to use as an asset for retirement consumption. People may use housing wealth for consumption through such financial mechanisms as reverse annuity mortgages. However, many retirees do not view housing wealth as an asset for retirement consumption. If housing wealth is not used to produce income, the level of savings in the above example and for the average American household is less adequate.

For some households replacement of all preretirement income may not be necessary to maintain the same standard of living. Expenses related to income production may lessen, saving for retirement may be stopped, and income taxes may be smaller. However, some expenses may increase, such as costs for medical care. Replacement of approximately 80 percent of preretirement income may be sufficient to maintain the same standard of living, but this will vary according to individual circumstances. Cutler reports that having assets of two to three times yearly preretirement income may be sufficient to replace 20 to 30 percent of it after retirement. This calculation assumes that people will live for 15 years after retirement, which is the average life expectancy at age 65. Those who live longer than expected face an increased risk of poverty due to such factors as a declining asset base and the inability to cope with inflation (Cutler 1996, pp. 125–149).

On average, people with a high school education or less have total assets at retirement age of about twice their median yearly earnings, including housing wealth. People with a college degree or above have average total assets at retirement age of about 3.5 times their median yearly earnings, including housing wealth. When housing wealth is not included, people with a high school education or less have average assets of less than their median yearly earnings. People with college degrees or above have average nonhousing wealth of approximately twice their median yearly earnings. If Social Security benefits replace 50 to 60 percent of the retirement earnings, income-producing assets of two to three times yearly income at retirement may be sufficient for a household to continue at the same standard of living (Cutler 1996, pp. 125–149).

The average total personal assets of Americans at the time of retirement may, under optimal circumstances, allow them to maintain their standard of living during retirement years when combined with Social Security benefits. A higher average asset level would be needed if circumstances or unexpected contingencies result in the need to replace more than 80 percent of preretirement income. Should the rate of personal savings or provision of employment-based pensions drop in the future, many Americans would experience a lower standard of living during their retirement years. Should the level of Social Security payments decline, many low-income people would not have sufficient savings to maintain a standard living at or above the poverty level.

Policy Development

Policy initiatives to preserve current levels of Social Security payments for low-income workers are essential to avoid increasing poverty rates. The passage of legislation that encourages personal savings and that supports higher rates of employment-based pension coverage would diminish the risk of inadequate income and impoverishment for all workers.

The medical insurance programs of Medicare and Medicaid work toward the prevention of poverty by supporting health maintenance for workers. These programs need to be preserved and expanded through continued policy development. Medicare insurance does not cover many essential medical needs, including prescription drugs and long-term care in nursing homes or similar facilities. Policymakers need to expand the Medicare program to cover the costs of prescription drugs. Legislators need to support the development of affordable and adequate long-term-care coverage through private or public programs to reduce the occurrence of poverty in old age. Such policy initiatives will help to deter poverty and to promote adequacy of income in times of disability or retirement.

References

Apfel, K. S. 1998. *Fast Facts & Figures about Social Security 1998*. Washington, DC: Social Security Administration.

Burtless, G. 1994. "Public Spending on the Poor: Historical Trends and Economic Limits." In S. H. Danziger, G. D. Sandefur, & D. H. Weinberg (Eds.), *Confronting Poverty* . New York: Russell Sage Foundation, Harvard University Press.

Cutler, D. M. 1996. "Reexamining the Three-Legged Stool." In P. A. Diamond, D. C. Lindeman, & H. Young (Eds.), *Social Security What Role for the Future*. Washington, DC: National Academy of Social Insurance.

Department of Health and Human Services. 1998. The 1998 HHS Poverty Guidelines. *Federal Register, 63*(36). Available on the internet at http://www.access.gpo.gov/su_docs.

Executive Office of the President. 1998. *The Economic Well-Being of Children: Economic Report of the President, 1998*. Washington, DC: Available on the internet at http://www.access.gpo.gov/ su_docs.

Executive Office of the President, Office of Management and Budget. 1998a. *Income Security: Budget of the United States Government, 1998,* Chapter 24. Washington, DC: GPO. Available on the internet at http://www.access.gpo.gov/su_docs/ budget98/maindown.html.

———. 1998b. *Social Security: Budget of the United States Government, 1998,* Chapter 25. Washington, DC: GPO. Available on the internet at http://www.access.gpo.gov/su_docs/budget98/ maindown.html.

House of Representatives. 1996. *401(k) Pension Plans: Many Take Advantage of Opportunity to Ensure Adequate Retirement Income*. (GAO/HEHS-96-176): Report to the Chairman, Subcommittee on Social Security, Committee on Ways and Means, House of Representatives.

Social Security Administration. 1997. Table 3.E3. Shares of money income from earnings and other sources for aged and nonaged families, 1995, *Social Security Bulletin Annual Statistical Supplement*.

———. 1998. Table 1.E1. Number and percent of OASDI beneficiaries also receiving federally administered SSI payments, by SSI category and type of OASDI benefit, March 1998. *Social Security Bulletin, 61*(2).

Steuerle, C. E., & Bakija, J. M. 1994. *Retooling Social Security for the 21st Century: Right and Wrong Approaches to Reform.* Washington, DC: Urban Institute Press; distributed by National Book Network.

U.S. Bureau of the Census. 1997a. *Health Insurance Coverage: 1997.* Washington, DC: Bureau of the Census.

———. 1997b. *Poverty: 1997 Highlights.* Washington, DC: Bureau of the Census.

———. 1997c. *Table A-2. Poverty Thresholds by Size of Family and No. of Children: 1997.* Washington, DC: Bureau of the Census.

Wolfe, B. L. 1994. "Reform of Health Care for the Nonelderly Poor." In S. H. Danziger, G. D. Sandefur, & D. H. Weinberg (Eds.), *Confronting Poverty* . New York: Russell Sage Foundation, Harvard University Press.

Chapter 5

Women and Minorities

Injustice anywhere is a threat to justice everywhere.
—Martin Luther King Jr.

Women and Social Security

Adequacy of Benefits

Social Security is an essential economic resource for retired women, disabled women, widows, and women with a totally disabled spouse. Women make up 60 percent of all retired Social Security recipients and represent 72 percent of all Social Security beneficiaries age 85 and above. They represent 98 percent of Social Security recipients who receive benefits as spouses with a child in their care. On average, women live longer than men, causing a gender imbalance in the rate of receipt of Social Security benefits. The average life expectancy of a woman at age 65 is 18.9 years compared with 15.6 years for a man (Social Security Administration, Office of Policy 1999, pp. 1–3).

Social Security is the only source of income for 25 percent of unmarried retired women, including those who are widowed, divorced, separated, or never married. In contrast, Social Security is the only source of income for 20 percent of retired unmarried men. Retired unmarried women receive 51 percent of their total income from Social Security compared with 39 percent for retired unmarried men. Unmarried retired couples rely on Social Security for 36 percent of their income. Almost 60 percent of elderly women are unmarried as compared with 27 percent of elderly men (National Economic Council, Interagency Working Group on Social Security 1998, pp. 1–19).

Women 65 years of age or over are less likely than men to receive a private pension and their pensions are smaller. Only 15 percent of the total income of elderly unmarried women comes from pensions as compared with 22 percent for elderly unmarried men and 20 percent for elderly married couples. Thirty percent of women aged 65 or older receive their own pensions as compared with 48 percent of men. The lower percentage of elderly unmarried women receiving pensions is partially explained by the fact that they are more likely to work part-time than men. In 1998, women represented 67 percent of all part-time workers and part-time workers are less likely to receive private pension benefits. Women are also more likely to drop out of the labor force to care for children, making it less likely that they will be eligible for a pension (National Economic Council, Interagency Working Group on Social Security 1998, pp. 1–19).

In the current economic climate women earn on average less than men. For full-time year-round female workers in 1997 the median income was $24,973. This compares with a median income of $33,674 for males. Inequality in earnings between genders declined in the period between 1981 and 1993. Women's earnings continually improved compared with men's earnings over this period. The trend toward gender equality in earnings should help to reduce gender differences in levels of Social Security benefits in future years. However, large discrepancies remain in income between genders (Social Security Administration 1998, pp. 183–189; Utendorf 1998, pp. 12–28).

For elderly unmarried women the median income in 1997 was $11,161. This compares with a median income of $14,769 for elderly unmarried men and $29,278 for elderly married couples. The lower wages of women provide private pensions and Social Security payments that are on average smaller than those of men. In 1997, the average Social Security payment for retired men was $860.50 compared with $662.40 for retired women (National Economic Council, Interagency Working Group on Social Security 1998, pp. 1–19; Social Security Administration 1998, pp. 183–189).

Without Social Security benefits women would be at high risk of falling into poverty in their old age or during times of crisis. The poverty rate among elderly women would be 52 percent without Social Security benefits. Elderly women have an overall poverty rate of 13 percent. The poverty rate for elderly men is 7 percent. For divorced women age 65 or over the poverty rate is 22 percent. It is 18 percent for widowed elderly women and 20 percent for never married elderly women. Married elderly women have a poverty rate of 5 percent (National Economic Council, Interagency Working Group on Social Security 1998, pp. 1–19).

Married women and men are eligible for spousal benefits during their retirement years. They receive a spousal benefit at age 65 equaling 50 percent of that of the high-earning spouse if their own earnings do not provide higher benefits. Social Security pays spousal benefits to 63 percent of aged female beneficiaries based on their husband's earnings record. Only 1 percent of aged male beneficiaries receive spousal benefits based on their wife's earnings record (National Economic Council, Interagency Working Group on Social Security 1998, pp. 1–19).

Divorced men and women may lose access to Social Security benefits and private pension income based on their former spouse's earnings record. Under certain circumstances divorced individuals can claim Social Security retirement benefits using their former spouse's earnings record. To be eligible divorced spouses must have been married for at least 10 years before their divorce. They must also be currently unmarried and 62 years of age or older. If they are eligible for Social Security benefits based on their former spouse's earnings record, the spousal benefits at normal retirement age are 50 percent of the retired worker's full age 65 PIA. The loss of Social Security benefits due to divorce may lead to impoverishment, especially for divorced women.

The survivor of a couple may experience impoverishment due to a decline in Social Security benefits and other income sources. Women are more likely than men to be the survivor. Survivors at normal retirement age receive 100 percent of the deceased worker's Social Security payment. However, the Social Security program reduces the survivor's income in comparison with what the couple received. A survivor of a couple who had income that was near the poverty level has a high probability of having his or her income level fall below the poverty line. Women in families that have a low social economic status have a higher probability of becoming widowed at an early age than those with a higher status. Therefore, it is more likely that widowed women will be impoverished as compared with married women (Steuerle & Bakija 1994, pp. 208–216).

Program Features

The 1935 Social Security act taxed the wages of all covered employees at the same rate up to a maximum amount of earnings per year. The formula for calculating benefits disregarded the gender of the recipient. The act disadvantaged women, however, in the selection of covered occupations. Covered occupations included less than 50 percent of all workers. Excluded occupations were ones in which women were most likely to work, such as those in education, government, agriculture, domestic service, and charitable nonprofit institutions.

The 1935 act had a regressive tax structure that required low-wage workers to pay a disproportionate share of their wages in Social Security taxes. Since women on average received lower salaries than men, this feature particularly

disadvantaged them. However, the formula for calculating benefits favored low-paid workers, which was an advantage to working women. Originally, the act provided no coverage for unpaid homemakers other than a small lump-sum benefit to survivors. The 75 percent of the women in the population who did not have paid employment did not qualify to receive retirement benefits or survivors benefits (Abramovitz 1988, pp. 248–266).

The 1939 Social Security amendments included provisions to provide benefits to the families of covered workers. These revisions gave increased protection to the security and stability of the American family. Under the 1939 Social Security act many women became eligible for benefits as the economic dependents of male workers. The act provided for paying supplemental grants to wives, widows, children, and to some parents of retired or deceased covered workers. These gender-specific amendments provided needed financial assistance to many women and families (Abramovitz 1988, pp. 248–266).

Regulations of the 1939 amendments institutionalized governmental support of gender-specific role behavior and certain types of family structures. The regulations rewarded married persons as compared with single persons. They favored families with a male wage earner and a female homemaker and encouraged women to be economically dependent on men (Abramovitz 1988, pp. 248–266).

Family protections provided by the 1939 amendments impinged on the principle of providing equal treatment under the law to all persons. In 1975, the Supreme Court in *Weinberger v. Weisenfeld* ruled that providing survivors benefits to widowed women caring for children but not to men in the same circumstance was unconstitutional. In the Court's judgment the practice violated the right to equal protection under the due process clause of the Fifth Amendment. This ruling overturned the principle that men's earnings are vital to family support while women's earnings are not. Other court cases followed that moved the Social Security system toward gender neutrality, such as *Cooper v. Califano* in 1978, *Yates v. Califano* in 1979, and *Ambrose v. Harris* in 1980 (Achenbaum 1986, pp. 130–139; Holden 1997, pp. 93–101).

Current Social Security regulations provide eligibility rules that do not discriminate by gender. Women, however, particularly benefit from some provisions of the Social Security program. Currently the program covers most occupations, including those in which women are dominant. On average women live longer than men, but Social Security benefit calculations do not reduce benefits to reflect gender differences in longevity. The benefit calculations index payments to reflect inflationary changes. This is particularly helpful to women because they have a greater longevity than men. The progressive benefit formula is particularly helpful to women since on average they receive lower salaries than men (National Economic Council, Interagency Working Group on Social Security 1998, pp. 1–19).

The Social Security program's provision of family benefits and the calculation of them rewards certain family structures more than others. Benefit calculations favor married couples compared with single persons. One-earner couples receive more generous benefits than comparable two-earner couples. The program favors families with stable long-lasting marriages over divorced families. Although the rules are gender neutral, they support cultural practices that maintain women's economic dependence on men (Abramovitz 1988, pp. 248–266).

Married workers receive spousal benefits that are rewards beyond what they would receive if they were unmarried and had the same earnings record. This conflicts with the principle of benefits being proportionate to Social Security taxes. The fact that two people need more funds to live adequately than one person provides a partial justification for spousal benefits. The fact that someone giving childcare should get credit for his or her work gives some justification for the policy of providing spousal benefits. The argument for such benefits based on need, however, is problematic. In fact, spousal benefits are inversely related to need. Since these benefits equal 50 percent of the primary worker's PIA, higher earnings result in higher benefits. Complete justification of the current policy is difficult based on either equity principles or the recipient's need (Steuerle & Bakija 1994, pp. 208–216).

Families with one earner rather than two earners receive higher benefits based on the same amount of average lifetime earnings. In two-earner households, the spouse with lower wages often contributes very little in additional Social Security benefits to the family. The lower earning spouse must earn enough to receive benefits on his or her own record that are more than one-half of the higher earning spouse's benefits to give the family any additional OASI benefits. These provisions reinforce a patriarchal family structure in which the man provides income and the woman raises the family. This model no longer fits the structure of many American families (Steuerle & Bakija 1994, pp. 208–216)

Eligible divorced individuals can receive spousal benefits based on their former spouse's earnings. These benefits are not related to the length of time that the marriage lasted beyond the 10 years required for eligibility. Benefits are not related to the accumulation of earnings during the marriage. The Social Security program computes spousal benefits for divorced persons in the same manner that they would be if the divorce had not occurred. Rules for determining eligibility and the amount of benefits for divorced spouses seem arbitrary and difficult to justify based on principles of equity. The justification of spousal benefits for divorced persons based on need is also questionable. The benefits are inversely related to need since higher benefits go to those whose former spouse had higher earnings. The current system rewards sustained marriage and punishes quick divorce. Social Security provisions relating to benefits for divorced spouses need to be reviewed and revised to promote equity and to consider issues of need (Steuerle & Bakija 1994, pp. 208–216).

The Social Security system does not give credit in benefit determinations for time spent on pregnancy leave or for time spent in providing unpaid family care-giving responsibilities. Benefit reductions in Social Security payments due to dropping out of the workforce to perform care-giving responsibilities can sometimes be substantial. Such benefit reductions particularly affect women because they are more likely than men to have care-giving responsibilities that require them to drop out of the labor force (Holden 1997, pp. 93–101).

For married couples, spousal benefits reward the low-income spouse who may have dropped out of the workforce for purposes of pregnancy leave or caregiving. However, these benefits are not specifically targeted to reward caregiving. Spousal benefits reward legal marriage. A spouse receives such benefits whether or not he or she engaged in family caregiving. Single parents who drop out of the workforce for purposes of caregiving do not receive such benefits.

The Social Security program computes benefits based on a person's indexed average earnings over a 35-year period. This method of calculation drops five years from the 40-year period of working years between a person's twenty-fifth and sixty-fifth birthdays. Use of a 35-year period rather than a 40-year period for benefit calculations is helpful to those who drop out of the workforce for purposes of care-giving. However, this method of benefit calculation is not targeted specifically to reward care-giving, but applies equally to everyone whether or not they had care-giving responsibilities.

Social Security policies do not specifically reward care-giving responsibilities that require a workforce dropout. This promotes gender inequity, since such care-giving responsibilities fall primarily on women in American society.

Policy Development

Policy-makers need to develop and adopt program changes that address issues of gender inequity in American society. They need to consider policy revisions that transcend the Social Security system and changes that relate specifically to it. It is important to develop and implement policies that move toward the elimination of wage and employment discrimination against women, which in turn, will help to address gender differences in the average level of Social Security benefits. Policy-makers need to develop and implement policies that will provide affordable and adequate daycare to reduce the need for women to drop out of the workforce to care for dependents.

The Social Security system could eliminate inequity related to caregiving by specifically targeting caregivers to receive Social Security earnings credits. Legislators could change the benefit formula to give credit for childcare. One method would be to reduce the number of years used to calculate average wages for those persons who drop out of the workforce for purposes of giving childcare. This approach is problematic because it rewards high-income earners with more credit for childcare than low-income earners. To avoid that problem policymakers might change the system to give some set amount of earnings credit to all spouses who drop out of the workforce for purposes of giving childcare. This approach would treat all childcare givers equally.

One proposed Social Security revision suggests that earnings credits be split between spouses to promote gender equity and reduce the inequities caused by the current policy of giving spousal benefits. The Social Security program would maintain a separate earnings record for each spouse, and each would receive Social Security benefits based on her or his own earnings record. Using this approach, the Social Security system would consider the total income for a couple as joint income with half the credit belonging to each spouse. For example, if during the year one spouse earned $50,000 and the other spouse earned $10,000, each would receive a $30,000 earnings credit.

Legal precedents support the fairness of earnings sharing for married couples. The Napoleonic Code serves as the basis for community-property laws in several states. This code specifies that the marriage bond gives each spouse the right to an equal interest in the earnings and property acquired during their marriage. In 1948, the Internal Revenue Service adopted the community property method of income taxation for married couples (Achenbaum 1986, pp. 130–139).

Many women would benefit from earnings sharing, and it would promote gender equity. One-earner couples, surviving spouses of one-earner couples, and divorced men would receive lower benefits than they do in the current Social Security system. Two-earner couples and surviving spouses of two-earner couples would receive more equitable treatment. Since some persons would gain and others lose, a change to earnings sharing would need to be phased in gradually. The earnings-sharing approach gives credit for the tasks of caregiving and homemaking. It provides an equitable distribution of earnings credits to each individual if divorce occurs (Steuerle & Bakija 1994, pp. 208–216).

Policymakers need to consider these and other approaches to promoting equity and fairness for both men and women in all types of family structures. The current debate on Social Security reform needs to focus on issues of gender equity in relation to solving the financial problems of the Social Security program.

Minorities and Social Security

Adequacy of Benefits

Racial groupings in the United States reflect an inequality in average wages. The 1992 annual mean of earnings per person for whites was $23,293 compared with $16,338 for African Americans and $20,317 for people in other racial groups. Mean earnings of African Americans declined compared with whites in the period between 1981 and 1993. This decline particularly affects African American men. Average earnings of African American men are declining compared with those of other groups. Average earnings of African American women are increasing faster than most other groups. An inequality in the level of earnings among racial groups underlies the phenomenon of differential levels of retirement and Social Security benefits. Social and economic policies that reduce earnings inequality need to be promoted (Utendorf 1998, pp. 12–28).

The poverty rates of various racial and ethnic groups in the United States are significantly different. The poverty rate for persons 65 years of age and over is 11 percent for whites, 22 percent for Hispanics, and 33 percent for African Americans. Social Security plays a primary role in deterring poverty for all retired Americans. Without Social Security 49 percent of whites, 62 percent of African Americans, and 61 percent of Hispanic Americans age 65 and over would live in poverty (Social Security Administration, Office of Policy 1999, pp. 1–3).

African Americans and Hispanics are less likely than whites to receive income from assets and from pensions during their retirement. In 1996, 32 percent of African Americans aged 65 and over received income from pensions. Pensions were a source of income for 20 percent of Hispanics aged 65 and over in 1996. In contrast, 43 percent of whites aged 65 and over received income from retirement plans. Social Security is important to minority groups because they are more likely than whites to rely on it as their only source of retirement income. Social Security was the only source of income for 16 percent of retired whites, 33 percent of retired African Americans, and 33 percent of retired Hispanics (Social Security Administration, Office of Policy 1999, pp. 1–3).

Racial minorities receive lower average OASDI payments than whites. In 1997, the average monthly OASDI benefit for whites was $713.70 compared with $562.80 for African Americans and $548.80 for persons of other racial groups. The average monthly OASI benefit in 1997 was $728.10 for whites, $578.30 for African-Americans, and $575.50 for persons of other racial groups. The average monthly DI payment was $607.00 for whites, $517.10 for African

Americans, and $495.00 for persons of other racial groups (Social Security Administration 1998, pp. 183–189).

The total value of retirement benefits that individuals receive from Social Security depends not only on the benefit level but also on the length of time that they receive the benefits. Different racial groups have different life expectancies at age 65. African Americans have a life expectancy of 15.6 years at that age. Life expectancy at age 65 is 17.6 years for whites, 21.2 years for Asians, and 21.2 years for persons of Hispanic origin. At age 21 life expectancies are 15 percent longer for white men than African American men and 9 percent longer for white women than African American women. High mortality rates lower the probability of receiving Social Security benefits and reduce the length of time that a person is likely to receive them. High death rates are related to income levels. Low-income people experience high mortality rates due to such factors as limited access to health care, poor diet, stress, hazardous employment, and high exposure to violence. (Social Security Administration, Office of Policy 1999, pp. 1–3; Steuerle & Bakija 1994, pp. 106–126).

Program Features

The 1935 Social Security act disadvantaged African Americans and other minorities in the selection of covered occupations. During the 1930s and 1940s many African Americans and other minorities had employment in agricultural and domestic service occupations. In 1930, 63 percent of all employed African American women worked in domestic or personal service jobs. In that year, 41 percent of all employed African American men worked as agricultural laborers. These occupations were not covered under the Social Security act until 1950. This placed African Americans and other minorities at a disadvantage in developing work credits to qualify for Social Security benefits (Achenbaum 1986, pp. 187–188; Abramovitz 1988, pp. 248–266).

Legislators eliminated the $122 minimum Social Security retirement benefit for insured workers in 1981. This revision disadvantaged low-income individuals, particularly those who did not qualify for Supplementary Security Income. Minority individuals with low incomes were negatively affected. Currently the Social Security program features a special minimum primary insurance amount that may be helpful to workers with low earnings and a steady attachment to the workforce for more than 10 years. Low-income African American women may be particularly helped by this provision due to their comparatively high labor force participation rates and long work records (Abramovitz 1988, pp. 248–266; Social Security Administration 1998, pp. 42–49).

The regressive tax structure of the Social Security system works to the disadvantage of low-income workers. The minority groups that have lower average income levels than the general population are particularly disadvantaged.

The payment structure for retirement and survivors benefits in the Social Security program provides higher total lifetime benefits for long-lived retirees and survivors. This works to the disadvantage of those minority groups with relatively short life expectancies. These groups could benefit from the Social Security reforms included in some privatization plans that allow accumulated retirement funds to be retained by survivors.

Some features of the Social Security program are particularly helpful to minorities. The progressive benefit formula is especially helpful to minorities because they have a lower average income than whites. The progressive benefit formula returns a higher proportion of preretirement earnings to low wage earners than to high wage earners. Social Security retirement benefits will replace 53 percent of preretirement earnings for low wage earners who retire at age 65 in the year 2000. This compares with a replacement rate of 40 percent for average wage earners and 32 percent for high wage earners (Social Security Administration, Office of Policy 1999, pp. 1–3).

The provision of disability and survivors insurance is particularly helpful to African Americans, who are more likely to receive disability and survivor benefits than whites. The Social Security Administration reports that African Americans receive 25 percent of the benefits for surviving children and 18 percent of the benefits for disabled workers. Only 13 percent of the U.S. population is African American (Social Security Administration, Office of Policy 1999, pp. 1–3).

Annual cost-of-living adjustments that protect against inflation are especially helpful to Hispanics and Asian Americans. Life expectancies for Hispanics and Asian Americans at age 65 are greater than for whites or African Americans. Inflation-adjusted benefits that do not erode in value over time assist Hispanics and Asian Americans to maintain their income level over the entire span of their retirement years (Social Security Administration, Office of Policy 1999, pp. 1–3).

The net combined results of Medicare and retirement benefits are progressive for those who retire after 2010, giving poor people larger absolute resource transfers than those received by the more affluent. This progressiveness is expected to increase over time, but is offset for African Americans, and perhaps other racial and ethnic groups, due to their shorter life spans in comparison with whites. The net effect of the interaction between shorter life spans and the increasing tendency toward progressivity is not entirely clear (Steuerle & Bakija 1994, pp. 106–126).

Policy Development

U.S. Social Security laws and regulations treat all racial and ethnic groups alike. The Social Security program needs to retain race and ethnic group neutrality in future policy provisions. Policymakers should consider, however, whether investment returns on Social Security taxes are fair to various racial and ethnic groups. They need to develop and adopt program changes that promote fairness and adequacy in the distribution of Social Security benefits to minority groups.

Legislators need to develop and enact policies that reduce prejudicial practices in American society. They need to adopt policies that are more effective in eliminating wage and employment discrimination against minorities. Such prejudicial practices reduce opportunities for minorities to develop wage credits that provide adequate Social Security benefits.

The United States needs to develop more adequate health insurance coverage for everyone and especially low-income persons. Policymakers need to consider ways to extend Medicare benefits to more men and women. They should develop provisions to increase the adequacy of Medicare benefits. Such extended health insurance coverage can potentially help to reduce the high mortality rates experienced by some minority groups. This in turn would promote a more equitable distribution of Social Security benefits.

Legislators need to consider the development of Social Security regulations that provide more adequate benefits to those with low incomes. Policies that benefit the poor will also be helpful to many minority groups who have lower average income levels than whites. Several different kinds of policy initiatives could be helpful in benefitting people with low incomes. Legislators could restore minimum levels of Social Security retirement benefits. They could modify Social Security's regressive tax structure to be less regressive. Social Security's benefit structure could be made more progressive.

Projections show that the Social Security system is moving toward increased progressivity through the redistribution of benefits based on current laws and demographic trends. However, not all of the benefit redistribution is directed to those with low wages. Policymakers need to develop and enact provisions that specifically target people with the lowest income levels to be the recipients of income redistribution. Such legislation would be helpful to the poor and to many minority groups (Steuerle & Bakija 1994, pp. 106–126).

References

Abramovitz, M. 1988. *Regulating the Lives of Women.* Boston: South End Press.

Achenbaum, W. A. 1986. *Social Security: Visions and Revisions.* New York: Cambridge University Press.

Holden, K. C. 1997. "Social Security and the Economic Security of Women: Is It Fair?" In E. R. Kingson & J. H. Schulz (Eds.), *Social Security in the 21st Century.* New York: Oxford University Press.

National Economic Council, Interagency Working Group on Social Security. 1998. *Women and Retirement Security.* Available on the Internet at http://www.whitehouse.gov/WH/New/html/womenrs.html.

Social Security Administration. 1998. *Annual Statistical Supplement to the Social Security Bulletin.* Washington, DC.

Social Security Administration, Office of Policy. 1999. *Why Is Social Security Important for Minority Groups?* Available on the Internet at www.ssa.gov/policy/pubs/bgpMinor.htm.

Steuerle, C. E., & Bakija, J. M. 1994. *Retooling Social Security for the 21st Century: Right and Wrong Approaches to Reform.* Washington, DC: Urban Institute Press; distributed by National Book Network.

Utendorf, K. R. 1998. Recent Changes in Earnings Distributions in the United States. *Social Security Bulletin, 61*(2).

Chapter 6

Family Policy

There is an eternal dispute between those who imagine the world to suit their policy and those who correct their policy to suit the realities of the world.
—Albert Sorel

Family Structure

The ability of families to function well is a key ingredient in the promotion of societal health and well-being. It is important that policymakers consider and understand families and their functions in relationship to selected demographic trends in society. The Social Security program is an important component among the multiple societal factors that influence the structure and functioning of American families. This chapter will explore the policy dynamics inherent in the Social Security system as it attempts to shape the structure of the American family and the family's ability to function. It will evaluate the need for policy changes in the Social Security system to correct program inequities and to reflect the changing structure of the American family.

The U.S. Bureau of the Census classifies households as family and nonfamily. Family households include families with married couples living together, with male householders where the wife is absent, and with female householders where the husband is absent. In 1997 the United States had 70,241,000 family households. Nonfamily households include those with single individuals and those with multiple unrelated people living together. The United States had 30,777,000 nonfamily households in 1997. A declining proportion of total households in the United States have married couples living together. Married couples living together constituted 78 percent of the total U.S. households in 1950 but only 53 percent in 1977 (U.S. Bureau of the Census 1998c).

FAMILY BENEFITS FOR THE LEGALLY

I WILL, BUT ONLY IF WE GET OASDHI FAMILY BENEFITS.

In 1997 the United States had 37,619,000 family groups containing the family's own children who were less than 18 years of age. All parent-child situations, whatever the living arrangement, are included as family groups. Sixty-eight percent of family groups had both parents living together in 1997 compared with 87 percent in 1970 (U.S. Bureau of the Census 1998b).

In 1997 the United States had a total of 70,983,000 children who were less than 18 years of age, excluding those living in institutions. Of these children, 68 percent lived with both parents. This represents a steady decline from the 85 percent of children living with both parents in 1970 (U.S. Bureau of the Census 1998a).

For people 15 years old and over in the United States the divorce rate is on an upward trend. The proportion of divorced men in the population increased from 2 percent in 1970 to 8 percent in 1997. During this period the proportion of married men declined from 66 percent to 58 percent. The proportion of divorced women in the population increased from 3 percent in 1970 to 10 percent in 1997. During this period the proportion of married women declined from 62 percent to 55 percent (U.S. Bureau of the Census 1998f).

An increasing proportion of married couples in the United States have both husband and wife in the labor force. In 1990 the United States had 53 percent of married couples with both spouses in the labor force compared with 57 percent in 1997. In 1990 the United States had 25 percent of married couples with only the husband in the labor force compared with 21 percent in 1997. Considering only married couples with children less than 18 years of age, the United States had 64 percent with both husband and wife in the labor force in 1990 compared with 68 percent in 1997 (U.S. Bureau of the Census 1998e).

The size of American families is in a downward trend. When including all households, the population per household was 3.33 in 1960 and 2.64 in 1997. When including only family households, the population per household was 3.67 in 1960 and 3.19 in 1997. Births per thousand women of ages 15 to 44 declined from 71.1 in 1980 to 61.4 in 1995. The percent of childless women of ages 15 to 44 increased from 36.7 in 1980 to 41.8 in 1995 (U.S. Bureau of the Census 1998d; U.S. Bureau of the Census 1997).

The average age of Americans is increasing. The median age of the population increased from 32.8 years in 1990 to 35.2 years in 1998. Between 1990 and 1998 the mean age increased from 35.2 years to 36.2 years. The average age is increasing both because of declining fertility rates and declining mortality rates. In 1900 a person's life expectancy at birth was 47 years. By 1991 it was 76 years. In 1991 the life expectancy for females at birth was 79 years and for males 72 years. An increasing proportion of Americans are 65 years of age and older. The percentage of Americans 65 years of age and older increased from 4 percent in/ 1900 to 12.5 percent in 1994. A Census Bureau estimate suggests that as high as 20 percent of Americans may be 65 years of age and older by the year 2050 (U.S.

Bureau of the Census 1998g; Economic and Statistics Administration, U.S. Department of Commerce. 1995).

Men in the United States retire at an earlier age than they did in the past. The retirement age for women remains stable over time. Seventy-five percent of men age 60 to 64 were employed in 1970 compared with 55 percent in 1993. Forty-one percent of men age 65 to 69 continued employment in 1970 compared with 25 percent in 1993. In 1970 approximately 37 percent of women age 60 to 64 were still in the labor force compared with 39 percent in 1993. Eighteen percent of women age 65 to 69 continued employment in 1970; this figure was the same in 1993 (Quadagno & Quinn 1997, pp. 127–131).

Program Features

The Social Security program encourages legal marriage by providing spousal benefits. It discourages early divorce. An insured worker's legally married spouse may be eligible to receive retirement benefits or benefits for caring for the worker's dependent children based on the worker's earnings record. An insured worker's currently unmarried divorced spouse of a marriage that lasted 10 years or longer may be eligible for retirement benefits based on the worker's earnings record. A widow, widower, or surviving divorced spouse may be eligible to receive survivors benefits or disability benefits based on the deceased former spouse's work record. Spousal benefits are available to a declining portion of the population reflecting the increasing divorce rates and the declining proportion of the population who are currently married in the United States.

Legally unrecognized family units do not receive Social Security benefits for one partner in the unit based on the work record of the other partner. If such units are caring for children, the program does not protect the childcaring function of one person in the unit while the other person works or when the worker dies or becomes disabled. This policy decision negatively affects both unmarried heterosexual family units and homosexual family units.

Family units of all types, including single-parent families, receive support through benefits provided for the dependent children of a worker who retires, becomes disabled, or dies. Children less than 18 years of age or in some cases 19 years of age may be eligible to receive monthly benefits. A disabled adult child of a worker who is retired, disabled, or deceased may be eligible for monthly disability benefits. To be eligible for such benefits the worker's child must be legitimate, illegitimate but acknowledged to be the worker's child, legally adopted, or a stepchild. The lack of legal marriage for a family unit negatively affects only children who would have been stepchildren in a legal marriage. These policy provisions seem to place a high value on caring for children regardless of the type of family unit. The provisions are congruent with the declining proportion of children living with both parents and the increasing number of children in other types of living arrangements.

Social Security policies discourage large families. Family benefits to spouses and children of retired, disabled, and deceased workers are limited to a maximum amount. Benefits for large families are not proportionate to their size. Families with more than two or three children receive reduced benefits per family member. These provisions are congruent with the downward trend in the size of American families.

The Social Security program determines benefits in a way that favors one-earner couples rather than two-earner couples. At a given level of lifetime contributions the two-earner couple will receive fewer monetary benefits than will the one-earner couple. The widow or widower of the one-earner couple will also receive greater benefits than will a two-earner couple with equivalent combined contributions of Social Security taxes.

For example, a one-earner couple in which the worker had an AIME of $3,000 would have a PIA of approximately $1,215.41 using 1998 bend points. If both persons retired at age 65, the worker would receive approximately $1,215.41 per month and the spouse would receive $607.70 per month. The couple receives a total of $1,823.12 per month plus an inflation adjustment. If the nonworking spouse should die, the worker would continue to get $1,215.41 per month. If the worker should die, the spouse would get $1,215.41 per month. In this example, if the spouse with no earnings took a low-paying job before retirement, it probably would not have produced larger Social Security benefits.

A two-earner couple with the same total amount of AIME would receive decreased benefits. A two-earner couple, where each worker had an AIME of $1,500, would each have a PIA of approximately $756.66. If both persons retired at age 65, each person would get approximately $756.66 per month. The couple would receive a total of $1,513.32 per month plus an inflation adjustment. This is $309.80 less per month than the amount the one-earner couple would receive. If either spouse should die, the remaining spouse would receive $756.66 per month. This is $458.75 per month less than the surviving spouse of the one-earner couple would get.

The policy favoring one-earner couples gives greater support to families with specialized roles in which one adult provides monetary support and the other adult provides home care and nurturing than it does to families with couples sharing these responsibilities. The policy may encourage fertility and protect childcare functions in an economic climate in which good paying part-time jobs are scarce and full-time jobs are often extremely demanding in time and effort. Preferential treatment for one-earner couples, however, seems incongruent with the increasing proportion of married couples with both husband and wife in the labor force. This policy disadvantages a majority of couples in the United States.

Inequitable treatment of one- and two-earner couples is gender neutral in that it allows either member of the family to assume either specialized role. Although the policy is technically gender neutral, women have traditionally played the primary role in home care and nurturing and continue to do so in many families. This is reinforced by the economic reality that men have on average better access to higher paid employment. Abramovitz believes that differential treatment of one- and two-earner couples devalues homemaker services by rewarding them at half the rate of the worker's income and attempts to preserve women's economic dependence on men (Abramovitz 1988, pp. 254–260).

American workers, particularly men, retire at earlier ages than in the past. Social Security affects the functioning of older families by encouraging early retirement since the program allows people to retire at age 62. Although the retirement benefits at age 62 are reduced, many people choose to retire then. The requirement that individuals prove retirement by passing an earnings test to receive benefits before age 70 encourages early retirement. Early retirement is also encouraged by requiring that a person continue to pay Social Security taxes when working past retirement age. Future scheduled increases in the normal age of retirement, increased penalties for early retirement, and increased delayed retirement credit will lessen the policy incentives that promote early retirement.

An actuarial analysis completed by Steuerle suggests that when considering all of the interactive factors, people receive a higher return on their investment in the Social Security program by retiring early. The incentive in increased retirement benefits is greatest for high wage earners and least for low wage earners. Steuerle's analysis shows a particularly high penalty in reduced return on investment in the Social Security system for those who choose to work past the age of 65. Even when the delayed retirement credit is increased to 8 percent per year, those who work past the age of 65 will still be disadvantaged. The longer people over age 65 work, the greater the disadvantage (Steuerle & Bakija 1994, pp. 219–224).

The Medicare program provides medical benefits to eligible beneficiaries and to people paying premiums if they are 65 years of age or older. Disabled workers less than 65 years of age receive Medicare benefits after being disabled for at least 24 months. A covered worker's disabled widow or widower age 50 and older becomes eligible for Medicare after being disabled for 24 months or longer. A covered worker's disabled children 18 years of age or older, if disabled before age 22, are eligible for Medicare benefits after being disabled for at least 24 months. Fully or currently insured persons with an end-stage renal disease of any age are eligible for Medicare benefits. Medicare coverage is not extended to other Social Security beneficiaries. The program promotes the health of covered families, but coverage needs to be expanded.

Family Functioning

Families traditionally perform the functions of begetting, socializing, and controlling children. They provide for the physical, psychological, and social needs of members. They produce and consume goods and services to maintain the family unit. Families, other social institutions, and societal factors play an interactive role in the performance of these functions. Policymakers need to examine Social Security's family policies to evaluate whether they are supportive or detrimental to families. It is important to consider whether Social Security policies should play a role in supporting certain types of family functioning.

Social Security policies influence the family function of producing and consuming goods and services by providing monetary and medical assistance to workers and their families in times of need due to the retirement, death, or disability of an adult working family member. The program's assistance also impacts other areas of family functioning such as the begetting children and the care of the physical, psychological, and social needs of family members.

For purposes of this discussion, a family is a social unit of two more members who are related by direct ancestry, adoption, legal marriage, or a long-term commitment to a marital relationship. The members must be engaged in some or all of the traditional family functions. Although most families would live in a single household, it is not necessary to do so to be considered a family. This definition encompasses extended families, nuclear families with or without children, single parent families, and gay or lesbian families.

Adequacy

Are Social Security policies adequate in their provisions for children and their caretakers? Although benefits may sometimes be adequate, the program is not designed to ensure adequacy for children or their caretakers. Benefits are intended to supplement needs in times of crisis. Caretakers and children receive 50 percent of a retired or disabled worker's PIA. They receive 75 percent of a deceased worker's PIA. Caretakers and children may receive less per family member in large families due to the maximum amount of family benefits. These monetary benefits do support families and family functions in times of crisis, but they do not necessarily provide sufficient support. Medicare benefits are not extended to caretakers and children unless they are disabled or age 65 or over. The lack of medical insurance is a significant gap in the adequacy of coverage.

Are Social Security policies adequate in their provision of assistance to workers and their spouses after a worker's retirement, death, or disability? The program supplements monetary needs rather than attempting to provide adequate benefits. Social Security benefits typically replace between 30 percent and 90 percent of a worker's former wages plus spousal benefits where applicable. Medical benefits are extended only to persons 65 years of age and over and to disabled persons. These benefits give support in times of need, but not necessarily adequate support.

Equity

Are Social Security policies equitable in their provisions for children and their caretakers? When treated equitably, people receive benefits that are proportionate to their contributions. Children and caretakers receive benefits that are proportionate to the worker's PIA. The Social Security program calculates PIAs to give greater benefits to those who have paid more in taxes, while favoring low-income workers. Benefits to eligible caretakers and children are not completely equitable because of the way in which PIAs are determined. This policy favors the provision of adequate monetary support for caretakers and children of low-income workers.

Are Social Security policies equitable in their assistance of workers and their spouses due to a worker's retirement, death, or disability? As mentioned in the preceding paragraph, the Social Security program determines PIAs to give greater benefits to those who have paid more in taxes, but with a formula that favors low-income workers. This approach disregards the principle of complete equity in favor of providing adequate monetary support for low income workers and their spouses. The family benefits are also inequitable because they give disproportionate benefits to married workers as compared with single workers.

Other factors need to be considered in determining the equity of lifetime benefits. Family type in terms of marital status and work roles (single, one-earner couple, two-earner couple) may affect lifetime benefits. The average medical needs of various groups of persons, taxes paid on benefits, the survival rate of various groups of persons, and the date at which one retires may also be related to lifetime benefits.

Steuerle reports on lifetime benefits when considering these factors. His analysis shows net lifetime benefits of persons in groups by wage level and family type. Those who retired in 1995 all received more benefits than the taxes paid by the employee and employer plus a 2 percent real interest rate, except the group of single high wage males. Net benefits were highest for the groups of average and high wage one-earner couples. The picture changes for those retiring in the year of 2030. Then all groups of low wage earners will still receive positive net benefits over contributions, with the group of one-earner couples receiving the highest net benefits. Groups of average wage earners will receive positive net benefits except single males. High wage earners will receive negative net benefits compared with contributions, except one-earner couples who receive a slight positive net benefit (Steuerle & Bakija 1994, pp. 124–125).

Social Control

Do Social Security policies attempt to control the form and function of the family? Policies of Social Security impinge upon the form and function of the family by extending spousal benefits only to legally married couples and by restricting them when divorce occurs before 10 years of marriage. They discourage large families by limiting family benefits to a maximum amount.

Social Security policies provide greater benefits for one-earner couples than for comparable two-earner couples. Favoritism toward one-earner couples encourages specialization in family roles. The reinforcement of specialized family roles may affect a family unit in a variety of ways ranging from encouraging fertility and protecting childcare functions to devaluing homemaker services and preserving women's economic dependence on men.

Social Security policies exercise control by requiring an earnings test for all beneficiaries except retirees over the age of 70. This test discourages employment. Social Security policies promote early retirement.

Policy Development

Policymakers need to consider revising some features of the Social Security program. People deserve to receive an equitable distribution of benefits after the subtraction of funds to promote adequacy for poor people and to protect the needs of children. Social Security policies that attempt to control family forms and functions are not justified unless scientific evidence shows that those policies promoted are beneficial or that those discouraged are detrimental to both family members and society. Monetary and programmatic considerations may sometimes provide a reasonable basis for making exceptions to these principles. Policy actions that are beneficial to society, but detrimental to certain affected individuals, may in exceptional instances be justified based on the overruling needs of society.

These value premises suggest the following policy revisions relating to family functioning:

1. Provision of an adequate level of protection for retired and disabled beneficiaries and their spouses needs to play a more decisive role in determining benefit levels. Providing average and high wage earners with positive net lifetime benefits while providing benefit levels that lead to impoverishment for some low wage earners is inappropriate.

2. Legislators need to adopt policies that determine the amount of Social Security benefits in an equitable manner for all people no matter what their marital status or composition of their family. They need to consider policy revisions such as an earnings sharing plan which allows spousal benefits to be gradually phased out.

3. Family benefits extended to divorced spouses need to be proportionate to the length of the marriage and/or amount of earnings during the marriage rather than being based on a requirement that the marriage last at least 10 years.

4. Family benefits not based on the beneficiary's earnings record might more appropriately be set at fixed amounts to give some degree of protection from poverty and to protect the needs of children and their caretakers.

5. The preferential treatment given to one-earner couples compared with two-earner couples with the same level of lifetime contributions to the Social Security program is inappropriate. The preferential treatment does not appear to be based on evidence that families functioning with two adult workers are detrimental to the welfare of family members. The policy is not equitable to retired, disabled, and deceased workers and their spouses.

6. The earnings test is needed because it serves to reduce the outflow of Social Security trust funds at a time when they are faced with declining future fund balances. However, Social Security policy needs to avoid the discouragement of employment in a system that may not provide an adequate standard of living for beneficiaries. Discouragement of employment may be detrimental to family functioning. Policies that will soften or eliminate the earnings test are desirable if financially feasible.

7. Regulations that encourage early retirement are undesirable. Early retirement does not necessarily benefit individuals or society and may be detrimental.

8. Medical insurance needs to be extended to the children and caretakers of children of retired, disabled, and deceased workers as well as to retired social security beneficiaries under the age of 65 and disabled beneficiaries without a 24-month waiting period.

These policy changes will strengthen the Social Security system by making it more adequate and equitable. They will decrease the controlling aspects of the program and give more freedom of choice to beneficiaries. The Social Security program provides important benefits to help and strengthen families. Human services professionals need to continually evaluate the program and promote revisions that will provide even stronger support for American families.

References

Abramovitz, M. 1988. *Regulating the Lives of Women*. Boston: South End Press.

Economics and Statistics Administration, U.S. Department of Commerce. 1995. *Sixty-Five Plus in the United States*.

Quadagno, J., & Quinn, J. 1997. "Does Social Security Discourage Work?" In E. R. Kingsom & J. H. Schulz (Eds.), *Social Security in the 21st Century*. New York: Oxford University Press.

Steuerle, C. E., & Bakija, J. M. 1994. *Retooling Social Security for the 21st Century: Right and Wrong Approaches to Reform*. Washington, DC: Urban Institute Press; distributed by National Book Network.

U.S. Bureau of the Census. 1997. *H1. Percent Childless and Births per 1000 Women in the Last Year: Selected Years, June 1976 to Present*. Washington, DC: Bureau of the Census.

——. 1998a. *CH-1. Living Arrangements of Children under 18 Years Old: 1960 to Present*. Washington, DC: Bureau of the Census. Available on the Internet at http://www.census.gov/population/socdemo/ms-la/tabch-1.txt.

——. 1998b. *FM-2. All Parent/Child Situations, by Type, Race, and Hispanic Origin of Householder or Reference Person: 1970 to Present*. Washington, DC: Bureau of the Census. Available on the Internet at http://www.census.gov/population/socdemo/hh-fam/htabFM-2.txt.

——. 1998c. *HH-1. Households, by Type: 1940 to Present*. Washington, DC: Bureau of the Census. Available on the Internet at http://www.census.gov/population/socdemo/hh-fam/htabHH-1.txt.

——. 1998d. *HH-6. Average Population Per Household and Family: 1940 to Present*. Washington, DC: Bureau of the Census. Available on the Internet at http://www.census.gov/population/socdemo/hh-fam/htabHH-6.txt.

——. 1998e. *MC1. Married Couples by Labor Force Status of Spouses: 1990 to Present*. Washington DC: Bureau of the Census. Available on the Internet at http://www.census.gov/population/socdemo/hh-family/htabMC-1.txt.

——. 1998f. *MS-1. Marital Status of the Population 15 Years Old and Over, by Sex and Race: 1950 to Present*. Washington, DC: Bureau of the Census. Available on the Internet at http://www.census.gov/population/socdemo/ms-la/tabms-1.txt.

——. 1998g. *Resident Population of the United States: Estimates, by Age and Sex*. Washington, DC: Bureau of the Census. Available on the Internet at http://ohrm.niddk.nih.gov/resident-population.html.

Chapter 7

Intergenerational Equity

Blessed are the young, for they shall inherit the national debt.
—Herbert Hoover

The Compact between Generations

When the Social Security program was introduced in 1935, it changed the nature of the financial responsibility of working adults for their elderly dependent parents in American society. The moral and legal responsibility to provide for the financial needs of dependent aging persons was largely shifted from the level of individual families to that of society. Instead of directly supporting aging dependent parents, working people began paying Social Security taxes to support the elderly. Those working in turn expected that they would be supported by the Social Security program during their retirement years. The program established a contract between generations that required each generation to pay taxes during its working years while giving it the right to receive benefits during times of adult dependency.

Vernon Greene presents another framework for examining the reciprocal contributions between generations. He discusses an investment model in which programs for aged persons and those for dependent children are perceived as an integrated reciprocal system. Working adults support children by paying the costs related to nurturing, medical care, and education. When a person's children enter the labor force, they benefit from the monetary capital buildup and knowledge generated from the past. The expenditures to support children reduce a working adult's personal consumption and ability to accumulate wealth. Investment in children provides the basis to claim a fair return through Social Security and Medicare benefits (Diamond, Lindeman, & Young 1996, pp. 158–162).

From the beginning of the Social Security program to the 1970s the media characterized older persons as poor, dependent, and deserving of governmental assistance. Since the 1970s the media have increasingly characterized older persons as prosperous, politically powerful, and receiving more governmental assistance than needed. The change in perception of older people in the mass media reflects in part the increasing proportion of funds in the federal budget devoted to programs for senior citizens. Current expenditures on programs for aging persons consume more than one-third of the federal budget and may grow in the future (Diamond, Lindeman, & Young 1996, pp. 158–162).

Government programs are a significant factor in poverty reduction among the elderly. Along with other sources of income they provide the average elderly person with a modest amount of prosperity compared with persons still in the labor force. For example, in 1996 the median household income for a married couple with no dependent children and with a 40–64-year-old householder was $58,656. The 1996 median household income for a married couple with no dependent children and with a householder 65 years old or older was $29,210 (U.S. Bureau of the Census 1996).

Both the early and the current stereotypical characterizations of older people are inaccurate and fail to reflect their diversity of characteristics. These stereotypical characterizations reflect a change in public perception of senior citizens. Policymakers have responded to this change in perception by critically examining publicly funded programs for older people. Policymakers are concerned about the fairness of the contract between working families and aged dependent individuals. One area of concern focuses on the question of whether the aged consume public resources at a level that deprives working families and children of needed governmental assistance. A related issue is whether the aged consume public resources at a level that prevents reduction of the federal deficit. Policymakers are also concerned about whether the aged receive benefits that are disproportionately large compared with their contributions to the Social Security system.

These are important issues for policymakers to examine. However, policy makers need to avoid resolution of these issues based on a stereotypical characterization of the elderly. Well-developed policy decisions on these issues require the examination of empirical evidence. Policymakers need to assess whether some elderly individuals receive benefits beyond those required to meet their needs adequately and beyond those that they have a legitimate right to receive based on their prior contributions. Social policy on these issues needs to support the provision of adequate resources to meet the needs of both dependent children and dependent elderly people.

Equity Determination

The pay-as-you-go method of financing Social Security transfers funds from the currently employed to the currently retired. This represents a net transfer of resources from workers to elderly dependent people. Considering whether the fund transfer is fair to both the working and the retired is important. Analysts often discuss this question as an issue of equity between generations. Although the concept of generation is vague, it generally refers to the time span and societal events during which a person or groups of persons lived.

If we ignore the broader range of resources that adults expend on children and consider only their contributions to and benefits from the Social Security system, how can intergenerational equity be attained? Equity evaluated under these criteria requires that on average people receive Social Security benefits that reflect their contributions plus a fair rate of return on investments. When people on average receive more Social Security benefits than their contributions plus a fair rate of return, the excess benefits are transferred from the current working generation to current beneficiaries. Such a transfer of funds would be fair to the currently working generation if they in turn received an equivalent excess transfer. Under expected future conditions the Social Security system cannot maintain continued payment of excess benefits. If on average Social Security beneficiaries continue to receive an excess of benefits, working adults will pay for them through an increasing tax burden per worker in each successive generation.

Policy analysts can determine whether individuals are receiving a fair value or their money's worth for investments in the Social Security program in several ways. One approach is to calculate the rate of return on investments using the present value of contributions and the present value of benefits. Analysts can assess money's worth by calculating the ratio of the present value of benefits to the present value of contributions. They can report the value of investments by the number of months that beneficiaries must receive benefits to be reimbursed for the present value of contributions. They can assess value by the net subsidy that reflects the difference between the present value of benefits and the present value of contributions.

Conclusions about intergenerational equity will vary depending on the rate of return considered fair. Since Social Security funds are invested in long-term government bonds, their expected rate of return is normally used in assessing intergenerational equity. The long-term expected real rate of return on government bonds is slightly more than 2 percent (Rejda 1999, pp. 132–134).

An unresolved equity issue is the determination of how to count employers' contributions in assessing the fairness of returns for individuals. Robert Myers asserts that employers' contributions should not be treated as assigned to the individual employee. He considers employers' contributions to be pooled benefits to support social adequacy. They can be used to provide social adequacy for people with low incomes or for other groups for whom payments need to be greater than the group's contributions. Myers points out that employers use their contributions to defined benefit private pension plans for similar purposes (Rejda 1999, pp. 132–134).

Labor economists generally hold that employers' contributions fall entirely on labor in the end. Employers shift the cost of their OASDI contributions by paying employees lower real wages and by charging higher prices. They argue that an underfunding of Social Security benefits would occur without the employers' contributions. They conclude that individual workers should receive credit for employers' contributions when assessing the fairness of returns for them (Rejda 1999, pp. 132–134).

The Social Security program is a defined benefit program that uses specified formulas to set individual benefits. It was not specifically designed to provide equity among or within generations. In fact, the program is designed to provide inequitable rates of return for some groups of workers. It has the dual purpose of providing a minimally adequate floor of protection for workers with low wages and providing some approximation of equitable returns for higher income workers. The dual purpose of the system requires a divergence from strict equity for all individuals.

Equity Studies

Some researchers examine equity between generations by completing empirical studies of historical data. This type of study allows the researcher to compare the payments and benefits of people who attained retirement age at various times. One source of such data is the Continuous Work History Survey maintained by the Social Security Administration. The survey uses a 1 percent random sample of covered retired workers.

Empirical studies show that retired workers who were born earlier have higher returns on taxes paid to the Social Security system than those who were born later. For example, a recent study by Duggan, Gillingham, and Greenlees reported that workers retiring between 1960 and 1968 received a real rate of return of 12.5 percent on taxes paid for and by them. Workers retiring between 1982 and 1987 received a real rate of return of 5.9 percent on taxes paid for and by them (Chen & Goss 1997, p. 83).

Chen and Goss explain that earlier cohorts of retired workers paid taxes at lower rates than was true for cohorts of workers retiring later. Pay-as-you-go tax rates increased because the number of workers per beneficiary gradually decreased over the years. Cohorts retiring later also paid Social Security taxes for more years before retirement than earlier cohorts. However, rising benefit levels also need to be considered. Benefit levels have gradually increased over the years. Adjustments of benefits for inflation were sporadic before 1987. Social Security recipients have received increased benefits each year since 1987 based on inflation in the economy. Some analysts believe that Social Security recipients are overcompensated for inflation. The value of medical benefits from the Medicare program have also increased considerably in the last few years (Chen & Goss 1997, pp. 73–83).

Hypothetical studies can project future returns from the Social Security system using life expectancy data, demographic characteristics, and economic assumptions. A study by Steuerle and Bakija reports the differences between the discounted amounts of total benefits expected and the total contributions that are or will be credited to workers reaching the retirement age of 65 in selected years between 1960 and 2030. When the discounted value of lifetime benefits exceeds the taxes paid for and by the worker plus a real return of a rate of 2 percent, the beneficiary receives a positive transfer of funds through the Social Security system. The study considers a positive transfer of funds to be a good measure of the redistribution of income (Steuerle & Bakija 1994, pp. 106–126).

Steuerle and Bakija indicate that when considering only the OASI program most individuals retiring before 1994, whatever their income levels or family types, received large positive transfers from the Social Security system. Retirees from future generations will continue to receive positive transfers but at lower levels. Some income and family types in the future will receive a negative transfer of funds from the OASI program. The decline occurs because lifetime contributions are growing faster than benefits. These results support the hypothesis that there is an intergenerational transfer of funds. Under current law it will continue in the future but at a lower level (Steuerle & Bakija 1994, pp. 106–126).

Medicare payments and benefits result in a positive transfer of funds from the currently employed to the retired. Currently individuals of most family types and income levels receive a positive transfer of funds. Projections show a continuation of positive transfers for low and average wage earners but a change to negative transfers for most high wage earners (Steuerle & Bakija 1994, pp. 106–126).

Medicare significantly adds to the benefits that persons receive from the Social Security system. The study by Steuerle and Bakija notes that projections of expected fund transfers in the Medicare program were difficult to make. Contribution amounts were difficult to determine since a significant portion of Medicare funding comes from general tax revenues. Projections of future payroll tax rates were unreliable due to financial imbalances in the program (Steuerle & Bakija 1994, pp. 106–126).

If net transfers include both the OASI and Medicare program, the combined size of the transfer amount is much larger than for OASI alone. Overall projections for the combined OASI and Medicare programs support the hypothesis that there is an intergenerational transfer of funds. Under current law this transfer will continue in the future, but it will decline for most average wage earners and will become negative for many high wage earners. (Steuerle & Bakija 1994, pp. 106–126).

Notch Issue

Policymakers modify the Social Security program periodically to preserve intergenerational fairness or fairness of benefits over time. Members of Congress created the basis for the "notch" issue when they initiated cost-of-living adjustments in 1972 to help Social Security benefits keep pace with inflation. Unfortunately the adjustments were not properly designed. Under the initial computation methods the benefit levels increased at a rate that could not be sustained. Congress responded in 1977 by revising the method for computing benefits.

Policy changes that rapidly alter Social Security benefit levels are likely to be perceived as unfair. The 1977 Social Security legislation that significantly changed the benefit formula provides a good example of such perceived unfairness. Those people reaching age 65 between 1982 and 1986 received sharply reduced benefits compared with those persons reaching retirement age immediately before them. After 1986, benefit levels began to rise again in relationship to inflation. Those people reaching age 65 between 1982 and 1986 are sometimes called the notch babies due to the drop in their benefit levels. The fairness of the reduced benefits for the notch babies became a social issue.

Legislators passed the 1977 Social Security amendments to correct benefit levels that were rising at a much faster rate than justified by inflation. Notch babies retired during the transition period that brought benefit levels back down to their proper growth path based on inflationary change. In relation to taxes paid plus a reasonable return on investments, the notch babies received more than their fair share of benefits. However, when individuals receive Social Security benefits that are sharply reduced from the immediate past, it seems reasonable that they would perceive themselves to be relatively deprived and that other people might agree with them (Steuerle & Bakija 1994, pp. 106–126).

Congress established a bipartisan Commission on the Social Security Notch Issue in 1992 to examine the treatment of recipients retiring during the notch years. The commission concluded that the notch babies were treated in a fair and appropriate way. They did not recommend any legislative remedy.

It is essential that policymakers consider the need to maintain consistency over time when designing policy changes to promote social equity. Abrupt changes that increase or decrease benefit levels create winners and losers depending on the time of retirement. Abrupt changes cause a perception of deprivation and unfairness. While legislation to take corrective action may at times be needed, the issue of the notch babies highlights the importance of gradual change.

Dependency Costs

The growing aged dependency ratio increases the concerns of policymakers about the ability of people of working-age to finance the Social Security program in coming years. The aged dependency ratio will continue to grow in the future, placing increasing demands on the Social Security trust funds. Transfers of funds between generations will become increasingly costly per worker under such conditions.

Assessing dependency from a broader framework, however, modifies the picture of the dependency costs placed on past, current, and future workers. Workers support both children and the aged. Ball and Bethell argue that the total dependency ratio is the most important factor to consider in assessing the manageability of the societal dependency costs. The total dependency ratio shows the combined number of young and old nonworkers per currently active worker (Ball & Bethell 1997, pp. 278–279).

Ball and Bethell report that the total dependency ratio in the United States in 1965 reached a high of 946 dependents per 1000 workers. The reported data were based on a report by the Social Security Board of Trustees. This report counts dependents as all individuals less than 20 years of age and all individuals 65 years of age and over. The 1965 dependency ratio occurred during a time when the baby boomers were children (Ball & Bethell 1997, pp. 278–279).

The total dependency ratio will reach a low of 653 dependents per 1000 workers in 2010 just before the baby boomers begin to retire. As the baby boomers retire the total dependency ratio will increase. By the year 2070 the total dependency ratio is projected to be 823 dependents per 1000 workers (Ball & Bethell 1997, pp. 278–279).

This view of dependency suggests that we will not be staggering under an unmanageable dependency load in the future. Resources formerly spent by working parents in raising children will need to be reallocated to programs that support aging parents. Although individuals and society may find such allocation shifts to be problematic, total dependency costs may be manageable.

The total dependency ratio needs to be interpreted in relation to the changing proportions of the elderly and children included. The total population of dependent individuals includes an increasing proportion of those who are elderly. In 1990 the population of dependent individuals contained approximately twice as many children as elderly individuals. In the year 2030 elderly individuals will exceed children in the population. After the year 2030 the number of elderly individuals per child will continue to grow (Price 1997, pp. 116–117).

Governmental programs for the elderly cost much more per taxpayer than do governmental programs for children. Except for educational costs and the costs of welfare programs to aid poor children, the dependency costs of children are largely covered by private expenditures. The dependency costs of the elderly are largely covered by governmental programs. The costs per recipient of governmental programs for the elderly are increasing. This is particularly true for health care (Price 1997, pp. 116–117).

Total future dependency costs might be interpreted as affordable when compared with the past and present. However, they will require a shift of funds away from private use. They will require more taxes to support increasingly costly governmental programs. The willingness of the American political system to pay for these programs remains in question.

References

Ball, R. M., & Bethell, T. N. 1997. "Bridging the Centuries, The Case for Traditional Social Security." In E. R. Kingson & J. H. Schulz (Eds.), *Social Security in the 21st Century* . New York: Oxford University Press.

Chen, Y.-P., & Goss, S. C. 1997. "Are Returns on Payroll Taxes Fair?" In E. R. Kingson & J. H. Schulz (Eds.), *Social Security in the 21st Century* . New York: Oxford University Press.

Diamond, P. A., Lindeman, D.C., & Young, H. 1996. *Social Security: What Role for the Future?* Washington DC: National Academy of Social Insurance: distributed worldwide by the Brookings Institution.

Price, M. C. 1997. *Justice between Generations: The Growing Power of the Elderly in America.* Westport, CT: Praeger.

Rejda, G. E. 1999. *Social Insurance and Economic Security.* (6th ed.). Englewood Cliffs, NJ: Prentice Hall.

Steuerle, C. E., & Bakija, J. M. 1994. *Retooling Social Security for the 21st Century: Right and Wrong Approaches to Reform.* Washington, DC: Urban Institute Press; distributed by National Book Network.

U.S. Bureau of the Census. 1996. *Table 4. Median Household Income by Type of Household: 1969, 1979, 1989, 1993, and 1996.* Washington, DC: Bureau of the Census. Available on the Internet at http://www.census.gov/hhes/income/mednhhld/t4.html.

Chapter 8

Reform

An indefinable something is to be done, in a way nobody knows how, at a time
nobody knows when, that will accomplish nobody knows what.
—Thomas B. Reed

Describing Reform Plans

Features

This chapter describes the policy choices suggested by reform strategies
and plans with regard to the following issues:

- How will the reform plan affect the distribution of benefits? Will benefits
  be means tested? Will only the selected individuals receive benefits? Will
  benefits be universally available?

- What benefits will be available? Will the proposed reform provide a
  defined benefit plan that specifies certain levels and types of benefits?
  Will it provide a defined contribution plan that specifies contributions but
  not specific benefits?

- How will services be delivered? Will services be delivered through
  governmental agencies or by private enterprise?

- What is the monetary cost in the proposed plan of startup costs, transition
  costs, operating cost, administrative costs, and borrowing cost? Will the
  costs of the proposed plan change over time?

- How will adequate finances be obtained? What fund-raising mechanisms
  and procedures will be used?

100

Values

This chapter considers the explicit and implicit values that the reform plans support. It describes the choices that the plan makes regarding the following types of value issues:

- ► To what degree does the reform plan support adequacy of benefits? How well does it support a person's preretirement lifestyle during retirement? How adequate are the benefits for poor people?

- ► How progressive is the reform (vertical equity)? Does the plan involve governmental redistribution of goods and services to the poor?

- ► To what degree does the reform plan promote individual equity by treating persons impartially and fairly? Are the benefits of the program related to a person's contributions? Do people get their money's worth from the program?

- ► How supportive is the reform of equality (horizontal equity)? Does the plan propose that every entitled person get an equal share of goods and services? Are people in equal circumstances treated equally regarding the taxes that they pay and the benefits that they receive? Are people treated equally whatever their gender, race, ethnicity, age, disabilities, marital status, sexual orientation, and generation?

- ► Is the plan supportive of a person's freedom of choice?

- ► How much emphasis is placed on social control of behaviors?

- ► Does the reform promote local autonomy or centralization of governmental functions?

- ► How much emphasis is placed on program effectiveness? Can the program be administered in an effective way?

- ► Does the reform promote program efficiency? Is the cost of the program low compared with the benefits of the program?

- ► Does the plan promote positive interaction with other systems and programs?

Goals

The review of reform strategies and plans describes the explicit and implicit goals that they support. The values held by planners give a basis for developing goals. The 1994–1996 Advisory Council on Social Security provided an example of a set of goals to be accomplished through reform plans. They developed plans to support the following six goals: (1) adequacy of retirement income, (2) insurance against unforeseen income fluctuations such as those caused by an earner's disability or death, longevity, or unplanned early retirement, (3) avoidance of market inefficiencies, (4) equity of lifetime Social Security taxes and benefits, (5) encouragement of private and aggregate national saving, and (6) strengthening the financial integrity of the nation's retirement income systems (Social Security Administration 1997, p. 245).

Reform plans may also support other types of goals such as: (1) redistribution of resources to the poor, (2) provision of freedom of choice for individuals, (3) equality in the treatment of all persons whatever their personal or social characteristics, (4) strengthening the financial integrity of the nation's federal medical insurance programs and (5) encouraging employment.

Program Evaluation

The evaluation of singular reform strategies and composite reform plans considers their potential positive or negative impact on the Social Security program and society. The goals noted above seem worth supporting because of their potential beneficial effects. The analysis evaluates reform plans regarding their provision of a means to achieve some, or all, of these goals.

Program Impact

The analysis describes the projected impacts of singular reform strategies and composite reform plans as compared with the impacts expected from the current Social Security program. It considers whether reform strategies and plans promote one or more of the following five features: (1) the provision of a feasible plan for promoting the long-term financial integrity of one or more of the Social Security trust funds or their replacements through other program approaches, (2) the provision of equitable benefits particularly between one- and two-earner couples and for persons of all marital statuses, (3) the provision of more adequate monetary benefits for low-income retired and disabled workers and their families, (4) the extension of medical benefits to the children and caretakers of children of current and deceased Social Security recipients, to Social Security beneficiaries under the age of 65, and to disabled beneficiaries without a 24-month waiting period, and (5) policy initiatives to encourage employment.

Societal Impact

The evaluation of reform strategies and plans assesses the potential positive and negative impacts that they might have on other programs and systems. How will the proposal affect the national savings rate, labor force participation, private retirement plans, or other economic functions? Will the plan support or negate functions of the family? Will the proposal enhance communities through the provision of citizen participation or in other ways? Will the proposal preserve or negate the preservation of individual rights and freedom of choice? What will be the magnitude of these impacts and how long will they last? How certain are we that these impacts will occur?

Feasibility

The evaluation of reform strategies and plans assesses the probability of their achievement of proposed goals. It evaluates a proposal's financial feasibility. It considers whether the mechanisms for finance are realistic regarding the assumptions made about cost and political acceptability. Will the financial mechanisms work in a market economy? Will the planned financial support be sufficient for the achievement of program goals? Will the resources be sufficient to provide the level of benefits specified in the proposal to all eligible beneficiaries?

The evaluation of the feasibility of reform strategies and plans also considers issues related to the administration of the program. Will a more complex and costly bureaucracy be required to administer the program? Will available personnel have the needed professional skills to administer the program effectively? Are there administrative barriers to delivering benefits only to eligible recipients in the right amounts at the proper time? How accessible will the services be to eligible beneficiaries?

Reform Strategies

Increasing Taxes

Features. One type of reform strategy increases Social Security taxes. An increase in payroll taxes of 1.1 percent for both workers and employers would restore the financial adequacy of the OASDI trust fund for an estimated 75 years. An increase of 1.65 percent for both workers and employers would restore its financial adequacy for the foreseeable future. Increased payroll taxes of 2.5 percent for both workers and employers would restore the financial adequacy of the HI trust for an estimated 75 years (Gramlich 1998, p. 44; Steuerle & Bakija 1994, pp. 54–55).

Reforms could increase the earnings subject to tax under the Federal Insurance Contributions Act (FICA). The most extensive revision of this type would provide no cap on the earnings that are subject to tax. A more modest revision would increase tax coverage from the current 87 percent to 90 percent of total covered taxable payroll. Currently the FICA specifies an earnings cap of $68,400 for Social Security taxes. Medicare has no earnings cap. The taxable earnings base for Social Security currently increases each year in relation to inflation.

Reform strategies could use future unified government budget surpluses for the Social Security programs. Actuarial projections of the number of future years that surpluses will occur and of the size of surpluses are subject to error. President Clinton used this approach as the primary strategy for increasing the financial adequacy of the Social Security and Medicare programs.

Increased general revenue taxes could finance projected deficits in the OASDI or Medicare trust funds. Some foreign countries use general revenues as a source for financing part of their Social Security programs. In the United States the Medicare SMI trust fund is currently financed in part through general revenue taxes. The SMI trust fund will need several additional percentage points of general revenue taxes in the future to maintain its financial integrity. Other trust funds could use this approach to finance their operations (Social Security Administration 1996, pp. 55–56; Steuerle & Bakija 1994, pp. 54–56).

Increased premiums for SMI coverage could restore part or all of the financial adequacy of that program. Premiums could be graduated in relation to income to protect the coverage of low income beneficiaries. The program initially required a premium equal to 50 percent of program costs rather than the current 25 percent (U.S. House 1997).

Higher deductibles for Medicare services would help to restore the program's financial adequacy. The use of higher deductibles is complicated by interactions with Medicaid. About 13 percent of those covered have secondary coverage through Medicaid that pays the copayments and deductibles. Higher deductibles would increase the costs to state governments for the Medicaid program (U.S. House 1997).

An increase in the taxation of Social Security benefits could provide additional support for the OASDI or Medicare trust funds. One proposal calls for taxation of all OASDI benefits that exceed what the worker paid in Social Security taxes. The reform would tax all benefits based on the employer's contributions. This would require an individual calculation of the amount of taxes paid. The proposed change would eliminate tax exclusion for those with low incomes. However, provisions in personal income tax laws would still exclude approximately 30 percent of beneficiaries including those with the lowest incomes from paying these taxes. Currently beneficiaries with sufficient income pay tax on up to 85 percent of their benefits. In 1993, tax laws allocated some taxes on OASDI benefits to the Medicare SMI trust fund. Some proposals call for using all of the taxes on OASDI benefits to finance the OASDI trust funds (Social Security Administration 1996, pp. 57–58).

Values and Goals Supported. Tax increases support strengthening the financial integrity of the Social Security programs. Increased taxes support the value and goal of providing Social Security and Medicare benefits that are adequate. They support the values and goals of the current Social Security system by maintaining most of the program's current policies. Increasing the earnings subject to FICA taxes and/or the use of general revenue taxes promote the value and goal of reducing the regressiveness of taxes to finance Social Security.

Projected Program Impact. Program revision through tax increases does not change the nature of benefits, distribution of benefits, or the way in which services are delivered in the Social Security program. Proposals for increasing taxes would restore some degree of financial balance and increase the confidence of the public in the actuarial soundness of the Social Security system. Restoration of financial adequacy would range from total to almost none depending on the degree and type of taxation.

The $68,400 cap on FICA taxes covers 87 percent of wages and salaries in covered employment. Immediately increasing the cap to cover 90 percent of total covered taxable payroll would improve the actuarial balance of the OASDI trust funds by approximately 22 percent of the estimated 75 year deficit. High-income workers could avoid some higher taxes through receipt of compensation as dividends or other payments that are not subject to Social Security tax. A higher cap would make Social Security taxes more progressive (Social Security Administration 1997, pp. 237–238).

Currently the HI trust receives part of the tax revenue that recipients pay on OASDI benefits. Some proposals call for redirecting this tax revenue to the OASDI trust funds. This change would provide funds to cover approximately 16 percent of the estimated 75-year deficit in the OASDI trust funds (Social Security Administration 1997, pp. 237–238).

Federal budget surpluses generated through general revenue taxes will probably not provide a long-term solution for actuarial soundness of the Social Security system. However, the use of federal budget surpluses would help to promote financial stability for the Social Security system and extend the number of years that the system would stay in balance. The use of general revenues to support Social Security programs might undermine their social insurance image in favor of a social welfare image.

Projected Societal Impact. Social Security tax increases would affect and distort the functions of the economy in ways that are not completely clear. If increased taxes support a higher overall savings rate in the United States, the economy would benefit. However, higher taxes may reduce individual savings and the government might continue to spend the generated surpluses on other programs.

Benefits do not increase under these reforms, but they become more costly. Future beneficiaries would receive less value for their contributions than do current beneficiaries. Labor costs would be higher for employers. Gramlich points to the possibility that higher Social Security taxes would serve as a disincentive to work and reduce the size of the labor force. However, this conclusion is controversial (Gramlich 1998, p. 46).

Some forms of increased taxation may negatively affect low-income workers. Plans that increase fees, deductibles, and taxation of Social Security benefits place additional costs on current beneficiaries, some of whom have low incomes. Many plans for increasing taxes place a greater burden on the generation that is currently working and may contribute to promoting inequities among generations.

Redirection of resources away from the Hospital Insurance Trust Fund would increase its financial instability. The HI trust fund has more severe and immediate financial problems than the OASDI trust funds. Although placing taxes derived from OASDI benefits in the OASDI trust fund seems logical and equitable, when viewed from a broader social perspective it would decrease one social problem by increasing another one in a proportionate amount.

Feasibility. Some degree of tax increase to finance the social security programs seems affordable and is likely to be politically acceptable. Tax increases of the amounts needed to provide long-term financial stability for all of the trust funds seem politically unfeasible and might have a negative impact on the economy. An increase in the earnings cap on FICA taxes would likely face high resistance from politically conservative politicians. Both the amounts of future unified budget surpluses and the use of these surpluses for the Social Security program are uncertain.

Tax increases are administratively functional and pose no serious administrative barriers. Startup costs and the administrative costs related to change are minimized with reforms that increase current taxes. The values, goals, and potential outcomes of proposals to increase taxes seem congruent with each other except as they negatively impact low-income workers. Tax increases represent a feasible means of providing at least a partial solution to the problem of providing adequate financial stability for the Social Security programs.

Reduction of Program Benefits

Features. Currently retirees receive full OASI benefits at age 65 and are eligible for reduced benefits at age 62. By the year 2027 retirees will receive full benefits at age 67. Congress could increase the funds available for Social Security by shortening the time span to move the normal retirement age to 67 years. It could secure additional funds by further increases in the age at which people are eligible to retire with full benefits. Congress could provide additional funds by increasing the age at which workers are eligible to receive reduced benefits due to early retirement. The age of eligibility for receipt of Medicare will remain at 65 years of age under current law. Congress could increase the financial stability of the Medicare program by increasing the age at which people become eligible to receive Medicare benefits.

A person's highest 35 years of earnings currently determines his or her Social Security retirement benefits. If a person's highest 38 years of earnings determined the benefits, it would on average slightly reduce an individual's benefit. This approach to reduction of benefits, however, might particularly affect female beneficiaries since women often drop out of the workforce to care for children. Combining the proposal to base benefits on the highest 38 years of earnings with an option to drop some years for child care might be a more equitable approach. Under such a plan a child caretaker could drop the years spent caring for children who were under a certain age when calculating benefits. This approach might be cost neutral or provide a cost savings while being equitable to child caretakers.

Currently beneficiaries get a raise in benefits each year based on changes in the Consumer Price Index. This compensates for the effects of inflation. Some economists suggest that the Consumer Price Index may overcompensate for the effects of inflation. One suggestion for changing this is to use the percentage rise in the Consumer Price Index minus one percentage point as a basis for the yearly increase in Social Security benefits. The Bureau of Labor Statistics estimates that the CPI overstates inflation by 21 percent per year. Some plans to cut Social Security costs propose that the CPI be adjusted by this amount each year for purposes of computing increases in Social Security benefits (Social Security Administration 1996, pp. 55–56).

A reform strategy called the "earnings-sharing plan" divides the total wages of a married couple between them. Each partner receives credit for one-half of a couple's total earnings. Under this plan each spouse would receive benefits based on the earnings credited to the couple. It would eliminate spousal benefits. The plan could be implemented by phasing it in over a long period. This would protect current beneficiaries and long-term participants from receiving significantly lower benefits. Some savings from this reform might be used to provide additional benefits for low-income beneficiaries. This would help to counter increases in poverty rates that might result from the application of this plan.

Medicare costs are likely to increase in the future as medical researchers develop expensive new medical technologies and as the demand for these new services expand. Currently Medicare uses predetermined prospective payments for specified diagnostic problems to control and perhaps reduce hospital benefits and costs. The program specifies levels of payments for Diagnostic Related Groups (DRGs). The Balanced Budget Act of 1997 reduced the rate of increase for future prospective payments of DRGs. It eliminated payments for days of stay in the hospital that exceed the mean for a particular DRG group. It initiated a prospective payment system for skilled nursing facilities that pays a per diem rate for covered services and established prospective payment systems setting predetermined rates of payment for defined units of service for home health care, rehabilitation hospitals, and hospital outpatient department services (Ways and Means Committee 1998).

The Balanced Budget Act of 1997 curtailed Medicare costs by reducing future capital expenditures for acute care hospitals and eliminated the indirect medical education costs received by teaching hospitals. These reductions provide cost-control mechanisms to promote the maintenance of reserves in the Hospital Insurance Trust Fund for the next few years (Ways and Means Committee 1998).

Congress could establish a global budget cap to control Medicare costs. It would specify a maximum expenditure for total Medicare spending under this approach. Congress would set spending targets for both fee-for-service Medicare expenditures and private health care plans. The plan would require the reduction of premiums and fees when projected expenditures exceed the budget cap (U.S. House 1997).

The Medicare program needs further reductions in expenditures or other approaches for promoting a positive fund balance to remain stable in future years. Medicare costs may be further controlled in the future by expanding the use of prospective payment systems and by establishing tighter controls on those currently in place.

Values and Goals Supported. On average current beneficiaries of OASDI and Medicare receive more benefits than provided by their tax payments plus interest. The value of individual equity suggests that beneficiaries should receive benefits that are proportionate to their payments and accrued interest. Controls to cut costs moderately through the reduction of benefits support individual equity for current beneficiaries. Cost-cutting promotes the value of equality and the goal of moving toward intergenerational equity by making benefits more congruent with payments.

Projected Program Impact. Since 1935, men have increased their life expectancy by three years and women by six years. Both men and women have projected further increases in life expectancy of three years by the year 2070. These increases suggest the appropriateness of an earlier change to 67 years as the age requirement for receiving full retirement benefits. It also appears to support further increases in the required age for receipt of retirement and Medicare benefits. However, increasing the age of eligibility for retirement benefits and for receipt of Medicare would serve as a hardship on persons with failing health or who lose their jobs due to age-related factors (U.S. House 1997).

If the age for eligibility for full retirement benefits were increased to 67 years by year 2011, the projected savings would amount to 5 percent of the 75-year actuarial deficit. If, after the year 2011, age of eligibility continued to rise parallel to longevity trends, there would be further savings of 18 percent of the 75-year actuarial deficit (Social Security Administration 1996, pp. 57–58).

An immediate increase in the number of years used to compute the indexed average wage from 35 to 38 years would save an estimated 13 percent of the 75-year deficit. The change would serve as an incentive to extend the number of working years and to postpone retirement. This change would negatively affect those with short work histories, including women who drop out of the workforce to care for children (Social Security Administration 1996, pp. 57–58).

If yearly Social Security benefit increases were based on a COLA that was adjusted downward by 21 percent per year as suggested by the Bureau of Labor Statistics, it would save an estimated 14 percent of the 75-year deficit. The inflation protection offered by the retirement benefits of the Social Security system is a desirable feature that is not typically found in other forms of retirement security programs. However, adjusting benefit increases to more precisely reflect inflation seems fair and promotes intergenerational equity (Social Security Administration 1996, pp. 55–56).

The earnings-sharing plan has the advantage of promoting equity within the Social Security system while reducing the benefits to be paid out in coming years. It promotes equity between spouses by crediting each with half the earnings. A spouse who stays home to take care of children receives an equitable amount of credit. If divorce occurs, each spouse retains a fair share of the credit for earnings. Discrepancies in benefits between one- and two-earner families are eliminated under this plan. One-earner couples would no longer receive disproportionate benefits compared with two-earner couples. The plan would provide more equity between married couples and single persons. It would reduce future payout and keep the Social Security system in balance for a longer period.

The expanded use of prospective payment systems provides a viable strategy for controlling Medicare costs. These systems need to be carefully monitored to ensure that payments are sufficient to purchase adequate medical services in the marketplace. Use of payment schedules that are too restrictive will reduce the quality and availability of services.

The establishment of a global budget cap would effectively control Medicare costs. Global budget caps have the potential disadvantage of reducing the quality of services or of making services unavailable. Providers with low payment schedules may decide to withhold services or to cut the quality of services. They may also attempt to find ways to select healthier beneficiaries as clients and withhold services to others. Beneficiaries might sometimes be forced to wait to receive services until Congress restores fees to a higher level. Global budget caps are more problematic in these respects than are prospective payment systems. Prospective payment systems provide a guaranteed base of payments that do not change at some arbitrary level of total expenditures. The guaranteed payment base stabilizes the program and makes it less likely that providers will arbitrarily withdraw services or force clients to wait to receive needed services.

Benefit cuts may work against the value and goal of providing adequate benefits. Plans for reducing OASDI and Medicare benefits increase the risk that some recipients with costly medical problems or with low income will no longer receive adequate coverage.

Projected Societal Impact. Benefit cuts may have a negative impact on poverty rates in the United States. It seems likely that cost of SSI and Medicaid would increase in the face of benefit reductions in Social Security and Medicare.

The current trend in the United States is toward earlier rather than later retirement. Earlier use of the requirement that individuals be 67 years old to receive full retirement benefits would help to counter this trend. Raising the age for full retirement benefits beyond age 67 would further counter the trend toward early retirement. Society would benefit from later retirements since a person's work life would be extended and his or her period of dependency in old age curtailed.

The earnings-sharing plan discourages having one principal earner rather than two in comparison with the current Social Security program. It reduces Social Security benefits for one-earner families. This seems likely to affect family life and structure by producing an increase in the proportion of two-earner couples in the workplace. The earnings-sharing plan could increase poverty rates for married retirees and their survivors if they had low incomes during their working years. To avoid this phenomenon, the plan could use some savings to increase benefits for those with low incomes.

Feasibility. The preceding plans to reduce Social Security and Medicaid benefits would be financially feasible and effective. Their political acceptability is uncertain. Benefit reductions pose a conflict between maintaining adequate benefits and developing a financially stable program with intergenerational equity. This conflict makes political acceptability more difficult. Control of expenditures through the extended use of prospective payment systems may require a more costly and complex bureaucratic system to administer the programs. However, cost savings should more than compensate for this additional administrative expense.

Increasing the Number of Covered Wage Earners

Features. The Social Security system faces financial difficulties in part because of a decrease of the number of wage earners per recipient. Congress could lessen this problem by allowing more working-age immigrants to come to the United States. This approach could potentially increase the funds flowing into the system without increasing taxes or decreasing benefits. The increased Social Security funds would be curtailed and offset by the costs of assimilation of new immigrants. Some gain would be offset by future benefit payments to immigrants.

Policymakers could increase Social Security revenues by extending coverage to all state and local government employees hired after 1997. Many state and local government employees are already covered under the Social Security system because of the federal government's compacts with state governments. The constitutionality of requiring state governments to participate in the Social Security system is a continuing concern. Recent Supreme Court decisions suggest an absence of constitutional barriers to compulsory coverage. The inclusion of this group of state and local government employees in the Social Security system would move it toward universal coverage. They are the last sizable group of workers who are not covered under Social Security (Social Security Administration 1996, pp. 57–58).

Values and Goals Supported. Allowing more working-age immigrants to reside in the United States would support the goal of strengthening the financial integrity of the Social Security system. The inclusion of all state and local government employees hired after 1997 would promote fairness by providing equal treatment for all citizens. It would support centralization of government rather than local autonomy. The change would support the goal of strengthening the financial integrity of the Social Security system.

Projected Program Impact. An increase of immigrants of working age in the United States would provide increased funds to support Social Security. The net impact would depend on the number of immigrants and their employment skills. Inclusion of all state and local government employees hired after 1997 would save money in the short term through increased tax contributions. Although more people would eventually be entitled to receive Social Security benefits due to this revision, the change would reduce the current long-term actuarial deficit by an estimated 10 percent (Social Security Administration 1996, pp. 57–58).

Projected Societal Impact. The societal impact of allowing increased immigration to the United States is uncertain. Some important variables that determine the impact of increased immigration include the readiness of economy to absorb additional workers, the personal and social characteristics of the immigrants, and the earnings skills of the immigrants. The inclusion of all state and local government employees hired after 1997 in the Social Security system would lessen the power and control of state governments.

Feasibility. The political feasibility of increasing the number of immigrants that come to the United States is questionable. Labor unions are likely to be strongly opposed to this plan. However, if the economy remains strong and labor shortages in key areas increase, the political climate may change in future. Increased inclusion of state and local government employees in the Social

Security system is likely be politically acceptable except to those politicians who oppose any proposal that might be interpreted as weakening state rights.

Using Funds More Productively

Features. Long-term government bonds are the primary method of investment for current fund surpluses. These bonds on average have a real interest rate beyond the amount of inflation of approximately 2 percent. As an alternative, the government could invest part of the surplus funds in the stock market to produce a higher rate of return. While investment in the stock market involves some risk, many financial analysts would consider it financially prudent to diversify investments between stocks, bonds, and other types of investments.

A number of proposals suggest the privatization of the Social Security system in part or in whole. Under such plans representatives of the Social Security trust fund or each wage earner would invest all or some portion of the individual's retirement tax funds in an individual retirement account. Beneficiaries would have access to these resources when they become eligible under current Social Security regulations. This approach allows participants to be less dependent on the decisions of politicians and bureaucrats. Most plans allow funds to be invested more diversely than is possible in the current system. Legislation could include certain restrictions on types of investments to avoid mismanagement of funds.

One approach to move the system toward partial privatization calls for an additional payroll tax of 1 to 2 percent. Participants would either invest these funds in a private account with certain restrictions or have them invested in privately owned but publically managed accounts. Individuals could withdraw these funds when eligible under current Social Security regulations. The plan would ensure that each contributor would have funds besides those provided by the current Social Security program.

A plan to provide vouchers to individuals to purchase private health insurance rather than continuing the current system of Medicare might increase the efficiency of the program. Those who favor such a plan argue that consumers would become more aware of costs and get more services for their money than is currently the case. Those who oppose such a plan believe that the government is in a better bargaining position than is the individual and that costs for the same services would go up under a voucher system.

Some Medicare beneficiaries currently receive services under managed care systems. Managed care systems are organized networks of health care providers that attempt to enhance the cost-effectiveness of the services provided. These systems provide the same services offered under the traditional Medicare system and sometimes additional services. The Balanced Budget Act of 1997 expanded the types of managed care systems that can be chosen by Medicare recipients through the Medicare+Choice program. These changes may encourage Medicare recipients to elect to receive services from managed care. If Medicare+Choice programs are popular and efficient, it is possible that Congress will decide to phase out the traditional Medicare option later as a means to control medical expenses.

The Medicare+Choice program that became operational in 1998 attempted to extend and strengthen cost controls for private health care plans by starting a new prospective payment system. This system moved toward establishing more emphasis on national rates of payment and less emphasis on local area–specific rates. This change was designed to be budget neutral. The flatter and less varied prospective payment system should encourage development of Medicare+Choice plans in areas where they are not currently available or viable.

Medicare+Choice organizations must accept eligible Medicare recipients regardless of health status and related factors during open enrollment periods. This restricts the ability of Medicare+Choice organizations to select only healthy individuals while leaving less healthy and more costly recipients on the traditional Medicare plan (Ways and Means Committee 1998).

Medicare+Choice recipients can elect to receive services from a qualified health maintenance organization (HMO), as was true before Medicare+Choice. An HMO is a managed care plan that provides medical insurance and comprehensive health care services for members who pay a regular flat fee. Medicare+Choice added provider-sponsored organizations (PSOs) and preferred provider organizations (PPOs) to the list of coordinated care plans that can contract to provide services to Medicare recipients. A PSO is a cooperative group of medical providers who control the delivery and financial arrangements for providing a contracted set of medical services. A PPO is a group of physicians and hospitals who contract with an insurance company or employer to serve a group of enrollees on a fee-for-service basis. Employers and insurance companies negotiate fees with PPOs at rates of that are usually lower than those charged to nonenrollees. Medicare recipients may also elect to receive services from qualified private fee-for-service plans. These additional options allow greater freedom of choice and increase the likelihood that recipients will choose to receive services from a coordinated care plan.

Medicare+Choice established a medical savings account option on a limited demonstration basis. This plan reimburses Medicare-covered services after a deductible of up to $6,000. It places the premium savings from the high deductible in an account for the beneficiary to use for noncovered expenses below the deductible if needed. It uses a prospective payment system to control costs (Ways and Means Committee 1998).

Values and Goals Supported. The investment of surplus Social Security trust funds in securities other than government bonds would be an attempt to promote the program's efficiency. The program would use surplus funds more efficiently if the funds could be invested to give a higher return than provided by government bonds. If successful, the revised investment strategy would support the financial integrity of the program.

If individuals make their own investment decisions, it would support the value and goal of giving freedom of choice. Individual investment accounts give greater assurance of individual equity on return on investments but could reduce support for the progressive features of the Social Security system. If private investment accounts are funded by additional payroll taxes, they would support a higher rate of national savings.

Both the use of vouchers and the provision of medical services through managed care systems have the goal of promoting greater efficiency in the use of Medicare resources. Greater efficiency in the use of resources promotes the financial integrity of the Medicare program. Both the provision of vouchers and the provision of more managed care options promote freedom of choice in relation to the type of medical insurance plan selected.

Projected Program Impact. If individuals assume the risk of investing their Social Security tax funds in securities other than government bonds, they may receive more or less adequate benefits than under the current system. They will have less insurance against unforeseen income fluctuations. Individual investment accounts do not provide insured returns and, therefore, provide less assurance of adequate funding at any given time as compared with the current Social Security system. If the government assumes the risk of investing Social Security funds in other types of securities than bonds, there is a high probability of a higher return and more efficient use of resources over time. The government could hire professional managers to promote prudent investment of funds and could invest funds with lower investment costs than individuals.

Private accounts give people greater assurance of returns that are individually equitable. Private accounts managed by either the government or individuals may work against the progressive features of the Social Security system. However, partial privatization while maintaining the current progressive features of the Social Security system is possible.

The use of additional payroll taxes for private investment accounts would not help the financial balance of the current Social Security system. Such taxation would not directly harm the financial balance of the system, but it might reduce the options to solve the problem.

Transition costs are a major barrier to privatization. Money diverted from current tax sources to individual accounts would not be available to pay benefits to current retirees. Privatization financed by current tax sources would accelerate the depletion of current surpluses. Privatization would require additional taxes or increased government borrowing to pay the benefits owed to current, and some future, retirees without a reduction of benefits.

Vouchers issued to individuals to purchase medical care may promote efficiency in the use of resources. If individuals could bargain better than the government in purchasing medical services, they would be more efficient in their use of monetary resources. However, the bargaining ability of people varies from person to person. The average bargaining ability of individuals may or may not produce more efficiency in the use of monetary resources. The Medicare program would need to supply vouchers that have low enough values to restrain program costs. This could place Medicare recipients in a position of not being able to purchase adequate medical care.

The addition of more managed care choices in the Medicare program potentially promotes efficiency in the use of resources. These plans typically offer medical services at lower rates than can be purchased by individuals in the open market. To promote efficiency the plans need to be carefully developed to curtail the ability of providers to select people who are likely have low medical costs while rejecting those who are likely to have higher medical costs. Otherwise, recipients with high medical costs will be rejected by private plans and disproportionately left on the roles of traditional Medicare. The actual payoff from using managed care options needs to be monitored and evaluated.

Medical savings accounts have the advantage of controlling program costs while encouraging comparative shopping and thriftiness by the consumer. The savings accounts are problematic since healthier persons who expect low medical costs are more likely to select them. Persons with high medical costs will avoid these plans because they will probably lose money. If medical savings accounts were universal, selection bias could not occur. Under a universal plan many individuals with high medical costs would be unable to pay for them.

Projected Societal Impact. People investing their own Social Security funds would have freedom of choice. It seems likely that persons would escape poverty due to their astute investment abilities while others would fall into poverty because of mismanagement of funds or bad luck. The overall societal impact is unpredictable. Total privatization of the Social Security system would curtail all redistributive features of the current system, resulting in an increased poverty rate in the United States.

If the government invests part of the surplus Social Security funds in stocks, it might become the largest stockholder in the nation. Government investments in securities other than government bonds might be considered a means to promote socialism because the government would in part collectively own the means of producing and distributing goods.

The proposal to add taxes of 1 or 2 percent to the Social Security system to invest in private accounts might increase the poverty rate in the United States. Low-income families could drop into poverty due to increased taxation. Private investment accounts funded by additional payroll taxes might support a higher rate of national savings, but such an outcome would be conditional on other investment decisions by individuals, corporations, and the federal government.

An increased opportunity for people to choose from a range of medical plans supports freedom of choice. If private plans provide a broader range of services at a lower cost, some individuals may be compelled to choose them rather than the traditional Medicare program. The choice of medical services within managed care programs may be more restrictive than those in the traditional Medicare program. Some people may feel that their freedom of choice has been restricted because they must choose a managed care program to get adequate medical coverage.

Feasibility. Government investment of Social Security funds in private securities faces considerable political opposition based on fear of government intervention in the decision-making process of corporations. If the government invests funds for private accounts, the program will have a moderate amount of additional administrative expense. It will need to keep track of these individual accounts and to monitor the investments. The proposal to have a wage earner invest her of his own funds in individual Social Security accounts is likely be more politically feasible in the current political arena. This approach would require less administrative expense since the Social Security program would not monitor the investments.

More productive use of Medicare funds is likely to be politically viable. The use of vouchers to purchase medical services would reduce administrative expense. Vouchers would likely be opposed by those who believe that individuals lack adequate bargaining power and fear that they would produce less adequate benefits. Managed care systems are administratively feasible. They are politically viable to the extent that they show the potential to use resources efficiently.

Composite Plans

The *Report of the 1994–1996 Advisory Council on Social Security* reports on the three Social Security reform plans that were most favored by council members. They include the Maintenance of Benefits Plan, the Publicly Held Individual Accounts Plan, and the Two-Tiered System with Privately Held Individual Accounts Plan. These reform options combine multiple strategies of reform to provide long-term financial stability for the OASDI trust funds and to accomplish other selected goals. They serve as alternative models for policymakers and politicians to consider in the debate over how best to resolve the problems faced by the OASDI programs (Social Security Administration 1997, pp. 23–34).

President Clinton in his State of the Union address on January 19, 1999 proposed plans to reform both Social Security and Medicare. He presented a revision of his Social Security plan and a more detailed Medicare proposal on June 28, 1999. The president's proposals seemed likely to play an important role in shaping the congressional debates around reform of these programs (Clinton 1999).

Maintenance of Benefits

Features. The Maintenance of Benefits Plan (MB) maintains the present Social Security benefit structure with minor modifications. It retains a defined benefit plan with benefits determined by a formula rather than proposing a defined contribution plan with set contributions but indeterminate benefit levels. The plan would change the benefit structure by computing benefits based on a 38-year period rather than a 35-year period. Council members suggested a possible alternative of a small immediate increase in employee Social Security taxes.

Employees would not pay federal income taxes on employer contributions to the Social Security trust fund. The plan would make the portion of an individual's Social Security benefits based on employer contributions federally taxable. The U.S. Treasury Department would credit these taxes to the OASDI trust funds.

Under current federal tax laws Social Security beneficiaries pay taxes on some of their benefits. The U.S. Treasury credits some of these taxes to the OASDI trust funds and some to the Hospital Insurance trust fund. The MB plan proposes that the law be changed to direct the U.S. Treasury to credit all taxes based on OASDI benefits to the OASDI trust funds.

The MB plan would make Social Security coverage more universal by requiring Social Security coverage for all state and local government employees hired after 1997. The plan would eliminate the option of state and local governments to exclude their employees from the Social Security system.

This plan would postpone Social Security payroll tax increases until 2045. Then employers and employees would pay a combined Social Security tax increase of 1.6 percent. Estimates show that the OASDI trust funds will need these additional taxes after 2045 to maintain financial stability.

Currently the Treasury Department invests all OASDI trust fund surpluses in U.S. government securities. Proponents of the MB plan suggest the investment of 40 percent of OASDI trust fund surpluses in stocks. They note that in the past government bonds have paid a 2.3 percent real return after inflation as compared with a 4.7 percent real return on stocks. An investment of 40 percent of surplus funds in stocks is conservative by private pension standards.

The president would nominate, and the Senate would confirm, a policy board to oversee the investment of trust fund surpluses. The board would operate under legislated fiduciary standards that would demand the investment of funds solely for the economic benefit of the Social Security program and not for other social or political objectives. The legislation would bar the voting rights provided by Social Security holdings or find other means to neutralize these voting rights. The MB plan suggests that further study is necessary before carrying out the proposal to invest surplus funds in stocks. However, this part of the plan must be implemented to meet an actuarial test of having a projected stable trust fund for the next 75 years (Social Security Administration 1997, pp. 23–34).

Values and Goals Supported. The Maintenance of Benefits Plan supports the development of long-term financial stability for the OASDI trust funds. It values maintenance of the OASDI program in its current structural form with limited modifications. The plan promotes adequacy of benefits at near current levels with only modest reductions. Although the increased taxation of Social

Security benefits would reduce program adequacy, it would also promote intergenerational equity by bringing the level of benefits for current beneficiaries closer to what they would receive based on contributions plus interest. The inclusion of all state and local government employees in the Social Security system promotes the principle of universal coverage. The proposed investment of surplus funds in the stock market attempts to make the program more efficient in the use of resources. Provisions to prevent government influence on corporate decisions reflect the value of maintaining capitalistic principles.

Projected Program Impact. If fully carried out, the provisions of MB plan would provide long-term financial stability for the Social Security program while maintaining benefits at near their current levels. Funds would be used more efficiently. Stochastic modeling shows only a slight increase in financial risk from the investment of 40 percent of surplus funds in the stock market when invested over a long perio (Social Security Administration 1997, pp. 23–34).

The program would come closer to universality of coverage under the MB plan. The MB plan would increase the equality of treatment of persons in society. It would promote intergenerational equity by taxing the benefits of current beneficiaries rather than raising taxes on current workers (Social Security Administration 1997, pp. 181–183).

Computation of benefits over a 38-year period rather than a 35-year period may be inequitable to female beneficiaries. In the United States, women are more likely to drop out of the workforce to care for children than are men. The change in computation may disproportionately reduce benefits to women as compared with men.

Replacement rates are the retirement benefits payable at age 65, or disability payments available on becoming disabled, compared with pretax earnings in the prior year. They show the percentage of earnings replaced by Social Security benefits. Projected replacement rates of the MB plan are essentially equivalent to those of the current Social Security plan (Social Security Administration 1997, pp. 36–56).

Internal real rates of return compare the present discounted value of future benefits to the present discounted value of taxes that will be paid to the Social Security system. Internal real rates of return can be expressed as the annual percentage rate of gain or loss that one receives from his or her investments through tax payments to the Social Security program. The internal real rate of return for the MB plan for single workers parallels that of the current law. For single workers, the projected internal real rate of return is lower than that of the

Personal Security Accounts Plan (PSA) discussed later in this chapter. One-earner couples fare better under the MB plan than under other proposed reforms. Two-earner couples fare generally less well under the MB plan than under the PSA plan for people born after 1970 (Social Security Administration 1997, pp. 36–56).

Projected Societal Impact. Government investment of funds in the stock market moves the form of government toward socialism. The MB proposal carefully limits direct government involvement in corporate affairs based on stock ownership. However, government influence on contract awards and on the enforcement of compliance with laws affecting corporations are not controlled and may be influenced by government ownership of stocks.

A requirement that all state and local government employees participate in the Social Security system would reduce the power of state and local governments. This policy would move the United States toward a more centralized form of government. However, the change would modify federal and state power relationships only in an incremental way.

Redirection of resources away from the Hospital Insurance Trust Fund would increase its financial instability. This change enhances the OASDI trust funds at the expense of the HI trust fund.

The MB plan would initially slightly increase the need for federal borrowing from the public as compared with the present program. Borrowing for purposes of the MB plan would generate funds to invest in the stock market. The plan would reduce the need for federal borrowing from the public after 2017 as compared with the present program (Social Security Administration 1997, pp. 36–56).

The projected 75-year OASDI trust balance in current dollars would be approximately 1 trillion under the MB plan as compared with a negative 2.5 trillion dollars under the current Social Security program. Projected OASDI spending as a percentage of gross domestic product (GDP) parallels that of the current law. Under the current law OASDI spending is approximately 4.7 percent of GDP and will rise to 6.7 percent of GDP by 2030 (Social Security Administration 1997, pp. 36–56).

Feasibility. The MB proposal appears to be based on sound financial projections and could provide long-term financial stability for the OASDI program. Financial results derived from investment in stocks seem less certain than those of other parts of the plan. They have the potential to be either much better or much worse than expected. The political feasibility of the plan to invest in stocks seems doubtful. Even with the proposed safeguards against government involvement in corporate affairs the plan is likely to be extremely controversial.

The plan's proposal to raise taxes may make its passage more difficult. Application of tax increases in the distant future makes the plan more politically acceptable. Tax increases are modest. This makes acceptance more politically feasible.

The MB plan seems administratively feasible. Although the changes would increase administrative complexity, this should not be a major problem. Costs for administering the program would remain at low levels.

Publicly Held Individual Accounts

Features. The Publicly Held Individual Accounts Plan (IA) would add defined contribution individual accounts to the current Social Security system. It proposes to fund the individual accounts through a 1.6 percent additional tax on the payroll. Funds would be held by the government. Individuals would have a limited choice of investments in various types of bond and equity index funds. When individuals became eligible for benefits, the government would convert the funds in their accounts to indexed annuities that will pay them a minimum stipulated amount per month or more. Individuals would pay taxes on their IA accounts either at the time of contribution or at the time of distribution.

Provisions of the plan accelerate the increase in the age of eligibility for full retirement benefits from 2027 to 2011. In 2011 the IA program would provide full retirement benefits at age 67 and reduced benefits at younger ages. After the year 2011, the plan proposes to increase the age of eligibility for full retirement benefits in correspondence to longevity trends.

The IA plan would reduce benefits through an adjustment in the benefit schedule. Beneficiaries would continue to receive 90 percent of their Average Indexed Monthly Earnings up to the first computational bend point that was $477 in 1998. Between the first computational bend point and the second computational bend point of $2875 beneficiaries currently receive 32 percent. The plan would change this to 22.4 percent. Beneficiaries currently receive 15 percent of earnings above the second bend point. The plan would change this to 10.5 percent.

The plan changes the computation of spousal benefits. Currently spouses receive 50 percent of the worker's benefits or the benefits based on their own working record, whichever is greater. Under the IA plan spouses would receive 33 percent of the worker's benefits or the benefits based on their own working record, whichever is greater. Surviving spouses currently receive 100 percent of the worker's benefits or benefits based on their own working record, whichever is greater. Under the IA plan surviving spouses receive 100 percent of the worker's benefits, 100 percent of benefits based on their own working record, or 75 percent of the couple's combined basic benefits, whichever is greater.

Some changes proposed by the IA plan are identical to those in the MB plan. Like the MB plan the IA plan would compute benefits based on a 38-year period rather than a 35-year period. It would tax all Social Security benefits derived from nonfederally taxed contributions. The IA plan would require Social Security coverage for all state and local government employees hired after 1997.

Values and Goals Supported. The Publicly Held Individual Accounts Plan promotes long-term financial stability for OASDI trust funds. It would give individuals more freedom of choice through the establishment of individual accounts with some investment options. Funds contributed to individual accounts would promote equity for individuals by returning benefits that are proportional to contributions plus investment appreciation. Increased taxation of benefits and other benefit reductions would promote intergenerational equity by increasing congruence between contributions and benefits for current Social Security recipients. The proposed individual accounts and the benefit cuts might encourage an increased savings rate in the United States.

The IA plan would maintain benefits at near their current levels for beneficiaries at all income levels. The proposed plan moves toward universal coverage by mandating the coverage of state and local government workers. It suggests changes in the computation of spousal benefits that will increase the equity between one- and two-worker couples and provide more adequate benefits for widows and widowers.

Projected Program Impact. If adopted, the IA plan has the potential to secure long-term financial stability for the Social Security program. The plan reduces compensation for middle- and high-income workers through adjustments in the benefit schedule used to set payments. However, it potentially would maintain compensation at current levels or above through proceeds from individual accounts that compensate for benefit reductions. This potentiality assumes investment results comparable to the average of those in other historical periods (Social Security Administration 1997, pp. 181–183).

Proposed increases in age of eligibility for full retirement benefits might have a negative impact on people who must retire early because of physical disabilities or age-related loss of employment opportunities. Although some of these people might be eligible for disability benefits, others would experience job loss from disabilities not severe enough to meet eligibility requirements.

Reduction of spousal benefits reduces the inequities between one- and two-earner couples. It could force some low income families into poverty. Surviving spouses would fare better under the IA plan with the option of receiving 75 percent of the couple's combined basic benefits. This option would particularly benefit the spouses of two-earner couples and might keep some of them from falling into poverty.

Projected replacement rates for retirees under the IA plan are roughly the same as those of the MB plan and those of the current Social Security plan. Under the IA plan disabled workers must wait until age 62 to be eligible to receive proceeds from their defined contribution accounts. Lack of eligibility to receive proceeds from a defined contribution account and changes in the benefit schedule reduce replacement rates. Replacement rates for disabled workers in the IA plan are a few percentage points below those in the MB plan and the current Social Security plan. However, lifetime benefits of the IA plan for disabled workers would be superior to those of the MB plan and the current Social Security plan. This superiority reflects the benefits received from defined contribution accounts after the age of 62 (Social Security Administration 1997, pp. 36–56).

The projected internal real rate of return under the IA plan is less than that of other proposed options for single persons, one-earner couples, and two-earner couples. Although the individual accounts should produce a higher rate of return on investments, the projected increase is not large enough to offset the reductions of other benefit cuts (Social Security Administration 1997, pp. 36–56).

Projected Societal Impact. Individual accounts give greater freedom of investment choice to workers. Government-managed accounts provide only a limited choice of investments but more choice than is possible under the current program. Progressive increases in the age of eligibility for full Social Security benefits may increase the average age of retirement in the United States and lead to a lower aged dependency ratio.

Individual retirement accounts and benefit cuts in the IA plan potentially will increase the savings rate in the United States. An increased savings rate strengthens the U.S. economy by providing more investment capital. Tax increases to finance the program and benefit cuts may negatively affect low-income families and produce higher poverty levels.

The IA plan would immediately begin to decrease the need for federal borrowing from the public as compared with the present program. By the year 2030 the government would need to borrow almost 20 percent less from the public than would be true under the present Social Security program (Social Security Administration 1997, pp. 36–56).

The projected 75-year OASDI trust balance in current dollars would be approximately 750 billion dollars under the IA plan as compared with a negative 2.5 trillion dollars under the current Social Security program. The IA plan would increase projected OASDI spending from the current 4.7 percent of GDP to 5.7 percent of GDP in 2030. Projected spending would then drop to approximately 5.2 percent of GDP by 2045 and stabilize (Social Security Administration 1997, pp. 36–56).

Feasibility. The IA plan includes a credible method of providing long-term financial stability for the OASDI program. Provision of individual ownership of investment accounts with some individual control of investment decisions shields the proposal from an image of moving toward a socialistic system of government. However, some political resistance may occur. Government-managed accounts might give the government some influence over corporate decisions. The proposal's benefit cuts and tax increases lessen its political feasibility. Tax increases for individual accounts, however, may be more politically acceptable than other types of tax increases due to the individual ownership of the investments.

Some degree of increased administrative complexity arises from the IA proposal. The plan requires a more complex bureaucracy with additional management skills to develop and manage individual accounts. Record keeping and communications related to taxation of benefits derived from formally nontaxed contributions would also increase administrative complexity. Although the increase in administrative complexity would be modest, administrative costs would increase.

Two-Tiered System with Privately Held Individual Accounts

Features. The Two-Tiered System with Privately Held Individual Accounts Plan (PSA) proposes to restructure the Social Security program to provide a basic floor of monetary support for beneficiaries plus benefits derived from investments in a personal security account. Under this plan the Social Security retirement and survivor's benefits would be transformed to a defined contribution plan without mandated specific benefits beyond those provided by the basic floor of monetary support. Disability benefits would unchanged from the current Social Security plan except for minor modifications.

Tier I of the plan provides a floor of $410 per month in 1996 dollars for beneficiaries who have 35 or more years of Social Security coverage when retiring at an age to receive full benefits. Workers with 10 years of Social Security wage payments would receive a half benefit of $205 per month in 1996 dollars. Beneficiaries would receive a 2 percent increase in benefits for each year of coverage beyond 10 until they reached the total floor benefit of $410 per month. Retired spouses would receive the greater of a floor benefit based on their own work record, 50 percent of the worker's benefits, or 50 percent of the full flat benefit. Surviving spouses would receive a floor benefit of 75 percent of the total benefits that would have been payable to the couple if both spouses were alive. The plan indexes Tier I benefits to inflation beginning in 1998.

Under the PSA plan disabled beneficiaries would receive benefits equivalent to the retirement benefits they would receive at age 65 under the present law. However, the plan would reduce disability benefits in correspondence to future increases in the age of eligibility for full retirement benefits. When people at age 65 received reduced retirement benefits, disability recipients would receive a corresponding reduction in benefits. The plan limits future reductions in disability benefits to 30 percent.

Tier II creates individually owned and managed personal security accounts (PSAs). Workers currently pay 6.2 percent of their salary in OASDI taxes. The plan proposes to use five percentage points of the taxes paid by employees to fund personal security accounts. It would use the 1.2 percent balance of the employee's OASDI taxes plus the 6.2 percent tax on the worker's salary paid by the employer to fund Tier I retirement benefits, spouses' benefits, survivor benefits, and disability benefits.

Individuals would invest PSA funds in securities of their choice within certain restrictions designed to promote the safety and liquidity of holdings. They would not be able to withdraw funds from their PSA accounts until they were 62 years of age. Regulations would not require conversion of accumulations to annuities at the time of a worker's retirement. Surviving spouses would receive the funds remaining in a PSA account at the time of their spouse's death. Remaining PSA account funds would become a part of the estate of a deceased worker without a surviving spouse.

On passage and implementation the plan would be fully effective for workers under the age of 25. The existing Social Security system would continue to cover all workers age 55 and older. They would only be affected by changes in retirement age, disability benefits, and benefit taxation under the new plan. The plan covers workers age 25 to 54 partially under the existing Social Security system and partially under the new system. Workers age 25 to 54 would receive a combination of their accrued benefits under the existing system and benefits they would accrue under the new system.

Tier II benefits would be fully funded through an individual's investment of OASDI taxes in a personal security account. This contrasts with the current pay-as-you-go system that uses an earner's Social Security taxes to pay for the benefits of current Social Security recipients. Benefits due to current and future recipients under the current Social Security system are only partially prefunded. Moving to a fully funded Social Security retirement system requires the payment of transition costs. The transition costs pay for the unfunded benefits due under the old system. The PSA plan proposes an OASDI payroll tax increase of 1.52 percent supplemented by additional federal borrowing to pay for transition costs. The government would issue bonds over a period of years worth $1.9 trillion in 1995 dollars to finance the transition costs. These bonds would be fully paid for in future years by the additional payroll taxes.

The PSA plan proposes elimination of the retirement earnings test when people become eligible for full retirement benefits. This proposed change applies both to benefits computed under the existing law and under the proposed Tier I benefit schedule. An earnings test would continue to apply to the receipt of early retirement benefits except withdrawals from Tier II personal accounts.

The PSA plan would tax all benefits derived from nonfederally taxed OASDI contributions. It would require Social Security coverage for all state and local government employees hired after 1997. Both the IA and MB plans propose these same changes. The PSA plan would credit all revenues from taxation on OASDI benefits to the OASDI trust fund. This revises the current practice of crediting some of these revenues to the HI trust fund. The MB plan also proposes this change.

As proposed in the IA plan, the PSA plan would accelerate the scheduled increase to age 67 for full retirement benefits from 2027 to 2011. After 2011 the age of eligibility for full retirement benefits would increase to keep pace with increases in average life expectancy for retirees. In addition, the PSA plan would increase the age of eligibility for early retirement benefits in tandem with increases in the age of eligibility for full retirement benefits. However, the PSA plan would not increase the age of eligibility for early retirement benefits beyond age 65.

Values and Goals Supported. The PSA plan fosters long-term financial stability for the OASDI trust fund. It supports adequacy of benefits by providing projected remuneration at levels that on average exceed those under the current Social Security system. Beneficiaries would receive an income from PSA accounts that reflects equity in relation to their contributions and their investment decisions. PSA accounts would provide more retirement equity between one- and two-earner couples than occurs under the present Social Security system. Tier I benefits also reflect an equity between one- and two-earner couples.

PSA accounts would provide more freedom of choice regarding investments than do other proposed reform plans. The plan encourages employment by increasing the age for early and full retirement. It also encourages employment by eliminating the earnings test at the age of eligibility for full retirement benefits.

The PSA plan de-emphasizes centralized government functions by placing more investment power in the hands of workers. The plan promotes universal coverage by mandating the inclusion of state and local government workers. This change promotes a more centralized system of government.

Projected Program Impact. The PSA plan would dismantle the current system of Social Security retirement benefits. It provides a financially feasible plan for securing long-term stability of the Social Security program (Social Security Administration 1997, pp. 181–183).

The PSA plan gives less certainty of a given benefit level. Its results would reflect the variance in investment skills of wage earners and market fluctuations in the value of securities. Participants in this system who lost capital through poor investment choices might face poverty and old age. Full Tier I benefits for an individual would be equivalent to 65 percent of the current poverty level for an elderly person living alone.

Proposed increases in the age of eligibility for early and full retirement benefits would be detrimental to those who must retire early because of physical disabilities or age-related loss of employment opportunities. Although some of these people might be eligible for disability benefits, others would experience job loss from disabilities not sufficiently severe to meet eligibility requirements. Elimination of an earnings test for people eligible for full retirement benefits would promote continued employment.

Projected replacement rates for retirees under the PSA plan are higher than under the present law and the other two plan options. Under the PSA plan disabled workers would not be eligible to receive proceeds from their defined contribution plans until they reached age 62. This would result in replacement rates for disabled workers that would drop to approximately 30 percentage points below those received from the MB plan and the current Social Security plan by the year 2036. After 2036, the replacement rates for disabled workers would stabilize. However, lifetime benefits of the PSA plan for disabled workers would be superior to those of the other proposed options. This superiority reflects the benefits received from the defined contribution accounts after the age of 62 (Social Security Administration 1997, pp. 36–56).

The projected internal rate of return under the PSA plan approximately parallels those of other proposed options for single persons and two-earner couples born before 1970. It would generally be greater than that of the other proposed options for single workers and for two-earner couples for people born after 1970. The internal real rate of return would generally be equal to or slightly above those of the IA plan and lower than those of the MB plan for one-earner couples (Social Security Administration 1997, pp. 36–56).

Projected Societal Impact. Increases in the age of eligibility for early and full retirement would increase the size of the workforce in the United States and lead to a lower aged dependency ratio. This would provide a larger tax base and lessen the burden on wage earners to support the insurance features of the revised Social Security system.

The PSA plan would make some reduction in program benefits, set up individual savings accounts, and raise taxes. These changes could have a positive impact on the national savings rate. However, the government would borrow heavily to finance the transition costs of this plan. The added federal debt would not be paid off until 2045. Increased government borrowing would reduce the national savings rate, particularly in the early years of the transition. This could have a negative impact on the economy. Proposed tax increases and benefit cuts might negatively affect low-income families and increase the poverty rate in the United States (Social Security Administration 1997, pp. 36–56).

Individual accounts supervised by wage earners promote freedom of choice. The redirection of resources away from the Hospital Insurance Trust Fund would increase financial problems in the Medicare program.

The projected 75-year OASDI trust balance in current dollars would be approximately 114 billion under the PSA plan as compared with the negative 2.5 trillion dollars under the current Social Security program. Projected OASDI spending as a percentage of GDP under the PSA plan would begin to decline from current levels in 2010 and level off at 3 percent of GDP by approximately 2050 (Social Security Administration 1997, pp. 36–56).

Feasibility. The PSA plan appears to provide a carefully planned method for providing long-term financial stability for the OASDI trust fund. It avoids direct government involvement in decisions regarding the investment of Social Security funds, which increases the plan's political feasibility. Reform plans that maintain the current Social Security system with minor modifications are likely to have a much greater chance of legislative enactment than those that propose major changes. Since the PSA plan would radically change the current Social Security system, its political feasibility seems questionable.

Application of the PSA plan poses several administrative difficulties. Keeping records and determining benefits for persons partially covered by two systems would require more bureaucratic capacity and seems likely to produce higher error rates than the current system. These additional tasks seem likely to produce higher administrative costs for the PSA plan as compared with the current Social Security program.

President Clinton's Proposals

Features. In 1999 President Clinton proposed using a portion of the current and projected unified budget surpluses to finance the costs of Social Security and Medicare. The value of the projected surplus was based on the optimistic assumption that the American economy will grow at the rate of 2.1 to 2.6 percent per year over the next 15 years. The plan projected that the unified budget surplus for the next 15 years would be $5.9 trillion. OASDI taxes account for $3.07 trillion of the $5.9 trillion surplus. The U.S. Treasury will issue $3.07 trillion in additional government bonds to credit the OASDI trust funds for this tax surplus. President Clinton proposed using the $3.07 trillion in OASDI surplus funds to reduce the $3.65 trillion of publicly held national debt. He would appropriate additional general tax revenues for the OASDI program in an amount equal to the interest saved by reducing the publicly held national debt. This was estimated to produce $543 billion, which the president proposed to invest in stocks and bonds. These additional resources were projected to keep the Social Security program financially sound until 2053 (Clinton 1999; Allen 1999, pp. 40–41).

President Clinton supported certain measures that would expand Social Security benefits. He would eliminate the earnings test that limits the amount that retirees can earn without losing social security benefits. The president advocated passage of some type of measure to reduce poverty among elderly women.

Although not specifically a Social Security proposal, President Clinton called for establishing universal savings retirement accounts. This plan would reimburse those individuals who establish and contribute to these accounts by giving them a tax deduction. It called for spending $540 billion of the surplus to fund these accounts. The government would give a tax deduction worth approximately $300 per person per year to invest in a savings retirement account. The government would match an individual's additional savings in his or her retirement account up to $350 per year for a total of $650 per person or $1300 per family per year (Clinton 1999).

President Clinton proposed to committing 15 percent of the unified budget surplus for the next 15 years to the Medicare program. This would give the Medicare program approximately $794 billion in additional funds. President Clinton proposed to use $118 billion of these funds to finance the coverage of prescription drugs for Medicare recipients. He proposed to use the balance of the funds to keep the Medicare program financially sound until approximately 2027.

The proposed prescription drug program would be voluntary. Enrollees would pay $24 per month when the program began in 2001. The premium would rise to $44 per month in 2008. The program would pay for 50 percent of up to $2,000 of the recipient's drug costs in 2002. The maximum would increase to $5,000 by 2008 (Clinton 1999; Bates 1999, p. 7).

The proposed Medicare reform plan would eliminate copayments and deductibles for the prescription drug program for single persons with incomes under $11,000 and couples with incomes under $17,000. The plan would eliminate copayments and deductibles for all participants for most cancer screening tests (Pear 1999, p. A16).

President Clinton's Medicare proposal would increase some costs to beneficiaries. The current $100 deductible for doctor's office visits would be adjusted upward with the rate of inflation. The plan would add a 20 percent copayment for most laboratory tests (Pear 1999, p. A16).

The plan would extend to 10 years the existing curbs on payments to health care providers that were a part of the 1997 balanced budget act. It would encourage competition among HMOs by allowing beneficiaries to keep 75 percent of the savings accrued from participating in HMO plans with lower costs. All HMOs would have to provide all of the benefits covered in the traditional Medicare program. They could offer additional benefits. The Medicare administrators would be given new authority to use competitive contracting to produce program savings (Pear 1999, p. A16).

Values and Goals Supported. President Clinton's proposals supported the financial integrity of both the Social Security and the Medicare programs. He favored increasing the adequacy of these programs through selected benefit increases. The proposal to eliminate the earnings test for retired workers would encourage employment. His plan called for more efficient investment of Social Security surpluses through investments in the stock market. The proposed universal savings accounts showed an intent to encourage national savings.

Projected Program Impact. President Clinton's proposal to use unified budget surpluses for the Social Security and Medicare programs provided a financial plan for maintaining their stability for an extended period of time. The plan provided an important first step toward ensuring the long-term financial stability of these programs.

The proposal significantly expanded the services covered in the Medicare program. An estimated 15.5 million Medicare recipients do not currently have any insurance for prescription drugs. Insurance coverage for drugs would provide these recipients with benefits that are essential to their health.

The ability of the plan to give financial stability to the Social Security program until 2053 and to Medicare until 2027 depends on the accuracy of projected assumptions. These projections are subject to significant error. Results may be either better or worse than expected.

The proposed plan will not sustain the financial integrity of the Social Security program for the 75-year time span normally considered the goal for long-term stability. The president would need to plan for the provision of additional resources to ensure the long-term financial stability of the Social Security and Medicare programs if his recommended reforms became law.

Projected Societal Impact. Significantly reducing government debt owed to the public would have a positive impact of the American economy. It would support the economic growth needed to produce the projected tax surpluses. The economy must grow at the rate of 2.1 to 2.6 percent per year in order for the tax surpluses to be realized.

The value of the projected tax surplus rests on the additional assumptions that tax rates will not be cut, that there will be no need for emergency spending, and that there will be future cuts in federal domestic spending. If these assumptions are inaccurate, the tax surplus may be much smaller than projected. The $2.83 trillion of tax surpluses that do not come from Social Security taxes would be particularly diminished if the assumptions are incorrect. If the projected surplus does materialize, the cuts in federal domestic spending could negatively impact the overall health and welfare of the nation.

President Clinton's plan to create universal savings accounts encouraged saving for retirement. The $540 billion that the government proposes to spend on this program would be placed in private savings accounts to be used for retirement. These funds would have a positive impact on the national savings rate. Money that individuals invest in these accounts would positively affect the national savings rate to the extent that it represents money that they would not have otherwise saved. Since universal savings accounts provide retirement benefits beyond the retirement benefits received through Social Security, they would not reduce the future funds that the government needs to support the Social Security program.

Feasibility. President Clinton crafted his Social Security proposals to avoid a requirement for increased taxation. This increased its political viability. The plan's proposal for government investment in the stock market represented a major political stumbling block due to the fear that the government will play a role in controlling the decisions of corporations. The plan's financial reliability was suspect due to the uncertainty of the projected economic growth and other conditions needed to produce the surplus tax revenues. President Clinton's plan was administratively feasible. It would require only a limited increase in the complexity and cost of program administration.

References

Allen, J. T. July 12, 1999. First, Assume A Windfall. *U.S. News and World Report, 127.*

Bates, S. 1999. Clinton: Let Medicare Pay for Prescriptions. *AARP Bulletin, 40*(3).

Clinton, W. J. January 19, 1999. *Address before a Joint Session of the Congress on the State of the Union.* Available on the Internet at http://www.whitehouse.gov/WH/html/19990119-2656.html.

Gramlich, E. M. 1998. *Is It Time to Reform Social Security?* Ann Arbor: University of Michigan Press.

Pear, R. June 30, 1999. Clinton Lays Out Plan to Overhaul Medicare System. *New York Times.*

Social Security Administration, 1996. Excerpt From the Report of the 1994–1996 Advisory Council on Social Security: Findings and Recommendations. *Social Security Bulletin, 59*(4).

———. 1997. *Report of the 1994–1996 Advisory Council on Social Security, Vol. 1.* Washington, DC: GPO. Available on the Internet at http://www.ssa.gov/policy/adcouncil/report/toc.htm.

Steuerle, C. E., & Bakija, J. M. 1994. *Retooling Social Security for the 21st Century: Right and Wrong Approaches to Reform.*

Washington, DC: Urban Institute Press; distributed by National Book Network.

U.S. House, 1997. *Economic Report of the President: Chapter 3. Economic Challenges of an Aging Population.* H. Doc 105-002.

Ways and Means Committee. 1998. *1998 Green Book. Section 2. Medicare* (DOCID: f:wm007_02.105). Available on the Internet at http://www.gpo.ucop.edu/catalog/green105.html.

Chapter 9

Political Action

If you're going to play the game properly, you'd better know every rule.
—Barbara Jordan

Target Selection

Human services professionals need to participate in the development and promotion of solutions for problems in the current Social Security system. They can use values, professional knowledge, feasibility estimates, and rationality to assist in the selection of targets for political action. They can promote fair and equitable solutions to social problems by engaging in processes of political advocacy. Such action can develop public concern and can organize political support to promote positive change.

Values and Ethics

Human services professionals have an ethical responsibility to pursue social change designed to promote social justice and social conditions that meet basic human needs. They need to focus their efforts on the development of social policies that prevent poverty, unemployment, discrimination, and other social problems. They have an obligation to engage in political action on the behalf of vulnerable and oppressed people.

To pursue social justice, human services professionals need to advocate for the enactment of legislation that will expand choice and opportunity for all people. They are obligated to promote social policies that give equal access to the resources, services, and opportunities that people require to meet their basic human needs. They have a responsibility to encourage the development and enactment of policies to support social equity and to protect the rights of individuals. Human services professionals need to support social action to prevent

136

and eliminate discrimination based on race, ethnicity, national origin, color, sex, sexual orientation, age, marital status, political belief, religion, or mental or physical disability.

Ethical principles give useful guidelines for selecting targets for social action. Such principles, however, often do not give sufficient direction to resolve all professional conflicts over legislative goals and courses of action. Human services professionals with different social perspectives, political viewpoints, and professional training may advocate very different goals and courses of action to uphold the same set of ethical principles.

Consider the following positions taken by professors in schools of social work in the United States. Tom Walz takes the position that Social Security is no longer viable and should become a voluntary program. Martin B. Tracy believes that Social Security should not be made voluntary. David Stoesz argues that privatization is a positive trend for the social services. Howard Jacob Karger thinks the negative consequences of the privatization of social services far outweigh any gains (Karger & Midgley 1994).

Kingson and Williamson argue against Social Security privatization plans. They assert that a privatization proposal such as the PSA plan detracts from community enhancing values. They believe that such plans undermine the basic insurance protection provided by the current Social Security system. They note that such a plan will shift risk from the government to individuals (Kingson & Williamson 1998, pp. 47–61).

Supporters of the PSA plan point out that it provides a basic-guaranteed floor of retirement benefits, spousal benefits, survivors benefits, and disability benefits for covered beneficiaries. Projected income replacement rates for retirees under the PSA plan are higher than under the present law. Projected OASDI spending as a percentage of GDP under the PSA plan will decline to 3 percent of GDP by approximately 2050. This makes the program more politically viable. These arguments would lead some human services professionals to disagree that the PSA plan undermines the basic insurance protection provided by the current Social Security system. While investment risk may be higher than under the current Social Security plan, this is balanced by higher projected returns.

Most policy proposals have both positive and negative aspects, making ethical choices difficult. Some courses of action may be clearly unethical. However, often ethical principles alone are inadequate to provide a satisfactory basis for choice. Additional evaluative criteria need be considered when selecting targets for political action.

Knowledge

Providers of human services must draw on professional knowledge bases when selecting courses of action for Social Security reform. They need to gather information on the results of scientifically based research and evaluation studies. It is important to consider the knowledge and opinions of professional individuals with expertise related to the effects of Social Security reform.

The quality of data will vary in reliability and validity. Human services professionals must carefully evaluate the knowledge provided by scientific studies and professional opinion. It is important to use the most credible evidence available in drawing conclusions and adopting policy positions. Professionals need to consider such knowledge along with other factors that inform and influence policy choices.

Feasibility

Targets for change and plans for attaining them need to be politically, financially, and administratively feasible. Political feasibility is driven by public opinion and the opinions of the politically powerful. Human services professionals must try to discern who thinks what in order to make informed choices about targets and plans for change.

Although the public has a good deal of concern about the problems of the Social Security system, most people do not broadly support increasing taxes or reducing benefits. A majority of people are not willing to postpone or eliminate cost-of-living increases in Social Security benefits. A majority of the public opposes increasing the age of eligibility to receive Social Security benefits (Baggette, Shapiro, & Jacobs 1995, pp. 420–442).

The public is not generally well informed about the causes of Social Security's financial difficulties and people do not understand the nature of the inequities in the Social Security system. This makes it difficult for many to accept the potential solutions for dealing with inequities and returning the program to a sound financial status (Blendon et al. 1997, pp. 111–116).

The concern that middle and younger age people have about the availability of Social Security benefits for them appears to drive the current political debate about the future of Social Security. Many people feel certain that they will not be receiving benefits equivalent to those currently being paid. Such concerns lead to debate between politicians and academics regarding the intergenerational equity of the current system. Public opinion, however, appears to reflect more concern about painlessly preserving current benefits than concern about issues of intergenerational fairness (Baggette et al. 1995, pp. 420–442).

The recognition that the affluent receive Social Security benefits has led to policy changes reflecting various forms of means testing. For example, the Social Security Reform Act of 1983 made some Social Security benefits subject to taxation. The Omnibus Budget Reconciliation Act of 1993 increased the taxes on Social Security benefits for those with high levels of income. Concerns about receipt of benefits by the wealthy will continue to be a focus of political debate in the future. A majority of Americans support increasing taxes on Social Security payments received by wealthy Americans, but otherwise oppose increasing the proportion of Social Security benefits subject to taxation (Baggette et al. 1995, pp. 420–442).

Human services professionals should consider the opinions of the politically powerful in determining the feasibility of Social Security action targets and reform plans. National politicians such as the president and members of the House and Senate must support legislation in order for it to become law. These policymakers are usually receptive to the opinions of those considered to have expertise related to the Social Security program. For example, the opinions of the members of the most recent Advisory Council on Social Security may play an important role in Social Security policy determination.

Associations concerned with the welfare of aging persons such as the American Association of Retired Persons may have considerable influence on the feasibility of Social Security reform proposals. Positions taken by professional organizations and political action groups that lobby and support the campaigns of politicians have a greater political impact than those of unorganized groups of people. The opinions of people more likely to vote, such as older people, have a greater impact than those of people who are less likely to vote, such as younger people.

Political activists need to assess the economic and administrative feasibility of possible courses of action. They can evaluate the economic feasibility of a course of action by considering the amount of funds that are, or are likely to be, available and by estimating its costs and benefits. Reforms are not economically feasible until funds are found for implementation. If estimated costs exceed the benefits for a given course of action, it is not economically feasible. Courses of action that provide the highest ratio of benefits divided by costs are the most economically feasible.

Estimates of administrative costs and complexity determine administrative feasibility. Change targets that are administratively simple and require low administrative costs have the greatest administrative feasibility.

Rationality

Professionals in human services need to use logical processes to assist in the selection of targets for change. Such an approach requires that they clearly specify goals and identify possible alternatives for achieving those goals. They must establish criteria for evaluating the identified alternatives. They must evaluate the alternatives with the specified evaluative criteria and select an alternative that maximizes the attainment of goals (Finsterbusch & Motz 1980, p. 24).

Selection of targets for change cannot be completely rational because of such factors as insufficient knowledge, conflicting values, intervening political processes, and insufficient resources. Although complete rationality in target selection is impossible, an approximation of the rational process is possible. Human services professionals can use processes of inductive and deductive logic when considering policy alternatives. They can approximate logical selection of courses of action based on available information. The courses of action suggested by logical analysis can be incorporated into the policymaking process.

Legislative Enactment

The process of enactment of Social Security reform legislation formally begins with the introduction of legislative proposals in the U.S. Senate and the House of Representatives. Legislators and their staffs prepare these proposals. Proposals receive a number and are usually printed in the Congressional Record. Often several legislators submit proposals on a given issue reflecting their own priorities and those of their constituencies.

The Senate assigns proposals on Social Security reform to the Finance Committee. The Finance Committee may consider such proposals itself or reassign the proposals to the subcommittee on Social Security and Family Policy. The House assigns proposals on Social Security reform to the Ways and Means Committee. This committee either considers the proposals or reassigns them to the subcommittee on Social Security.

The subcommittee or committee members discuss the merits of a proposal and revise it to reflect their position and concerns. They call this process "marking-up" the proposal. A committee typically hears testimony from experts, lobbyists, and representatives of groups interested in influencing Social Security reform legislation. It carefully considers the budgetary implications of a proposed reform. Legislative proposals on Social Security reform need to be passed by the Finance Committee to be considered for passage in the Senate. Proposals need to be passed by the Ways and Means Committee to be considered for passage in the House.

To become law, Social Security reform legislation must be passed by both the Senate and House. Each of these legislative bodies debates, listens to testimony, considers amendments, and votes on the committee approved Social Security reforms. Differences in reform measures passed by both the House and Senate must be resolved by a conference committee. If the resolution of the conference committee is acceptable to both houses of Congress, the legislative proposal is sent to the president. The president either signs or vetoes the legislation. If vetoed by the president, the legislation could still become law if it is then approved by two-thirds of the members of each legislative chamber.

The legislative process places significant barriers on the passage of Social Security reform. In the last 20 years congressional committees approved only 10 percent of all of the bills of any type that legislators introduced. Only 5 percent of all of the bills that legislators introduced became law (Karger & Stoesz 1998, p. 228).

Advocacy

Human services professionals practice advocacy by acting on the behalf of the poor, the oppressed, and those who are not receiving just treatment from society. They may advocate to promote social justice for both clients and nonclients. After selecting a plan for reform of the Social Security system that promotes social justice, human services professionals can participate in advocacy processes to promote legislative enactment. The degree of a human services professional's involvement in advocacy processes to reform the Social Security system will vary depending on the professional's job description, expertise, clientele, and interest.

Individual human service professionals, substantive committees, commissions, agencies, professional organizations, political action committees, and various other interest groups and associations engage in legislative advocacy. Individuals and organizations use their persuasive ability, expertise, political capital, and campaign contributions to influence key political decision makers on proposals for Social Security reform. Human services professionals should recognize that their training, experience, and knowledge provide a potentially powerful tool that can be exercised to influence legislative policy. The primary task is to persuade political decision makers to use their influence and voting power to support the targeted reform.

Community Support

Human services professionals may wish to join advocacy groups that support the type of reform policies that they want to promote. The American Association of Retired Persons, Gray Panthers, National Committee to Preserve Social Security and Medicare, and National Council on the Aging, Inc. are among those advocacy groups that will be interested in influencing the course of Social Security reform (Brueggemann 1996, p. 414).

Existing organizations may not effectively represent the policy position supported by a human services professional. Human services professionals may need to develop an organization or a coalition of individuals and organizations to support targeted legislative action. Coalitions are built through such activities as education, publicity, conferences, networking, and campaigns for commitment.

Organizations and coalitions attempt to support their legislative agenda by taking political action. Their capacity to influence the political process expands with increased membership size, wealth, and professional expertise. They attempt to influence legislators and the legislative process through lobbying, litigation, donations to political candidates, and media campaigns.

Lobbying

Individuals and organizational representatives can engage in face-to-face lobbying when meeting with legislators or legislative aides. Such lobbying with legislators on the committees and subcommittees that act on Social Security legislation gives direct access to those who will play a key role in determining legislative action or inaction. Careful preparation for such meetings will ensure maximum impact. Legislators will want to know the costs and benefits of proposed changes. They will want to know about the presenter's expertise. Legislators will be interested in the presenter's political power base and willingness to use it to support them. Summaries of research findings and other supportive documentation may be helpful. Presentations should be factual and succinct. A followup thank-you letter that gives a synopsis of the lobbyist's position and the legislator's response is appropriate.

Lobbyists may be invited to testify before congressional committees that deal with Social Security reform. Congressional committees usually invite lobbyists to testify because of their known expertise or because they represent an influential interest group. Presentations should be interesting, brief, and informative. Presenters should discuss the values that they support and goals that they hope to attain. They should summarize the features of their proposed reform, its cost, its economic feasibility, its administrative feasibility, and its anticipated impact. They should be prepared to respond factually and persuasively to those who oppose their position.

Individuals, commissions, think tanks, and interest groups can lobby legislators by sending reports of legislative analysis and relevant research. As in other types of lobbying efforts, the reports should be persuasive and succinct. They should contain similar information to what would be presented when lobbying through testimony or face-to-face. Reports normally contain more factual detail and information about the reliability and validity of findings and conclusions than the lobbyist would present when using other approaches.

Organizations and individuals can lobby legislators through email and letter writing. Messages should be short, concise, and credible. Messages need to describe clearly the action that should be taken or the position that should be supported. Describe and document the reasons for the recommended action. Indicate your professional and organizational credentials. Individually written letters or email messages are the most persuasive and effective. Form letters can be effective when received from a large number of individuals. Petitions signed by many people may also be persuasive.

Individuals and organizations may use telephone messages to lobby legislators. Telephone messages to support a position are typically only a few sentences long. They indicate briefly the bill or action that should be supported. Callers should leave their name, address, and phone number. Individuals and representatives of organizations who have a personal relationship with a legislator or influential credentials can use telephone conversations with a legislator to lobby for a position in a more lengthy and substantial way.

References

Baggette, J., Shapiro, R. Y., & Jacobs, L. R. 1995. Social Security—An Update. *Public Opinion Quarterly, 59*(3).

Blendon, R. J., Benson, J. M., Brodie, M., Brossard, M., Altman, D. E., & Morin, R. 1997. What Do Americans Know about Entitlements? *Health Affairs, 16*(5).

Brueggemann, W. G. 1996. *The Practice of Macro Social Work.* Chicago: Nelson-Hall.

Finsterbusch, K., & Motz, A. B. 1980. *Social Research for Policy Decisions.* Belmont, CA: Wadsworth Publishing Company.

Karger, H. J., & Midgley, J. (Eds.). 1994. *Controversial Issues in Social Policy.* Boston: Allyn & Bacon.

Karger, H. J., & Stoesz, D. 1998. *American Social Welfare Policy.* (3rd ed.). New York: Addison Wesley Longman.

Kingson, E. R., & Williamson, J. B. 1998. Understanding the Debate over the Privatization of Social Security. *Journal of Sociology and Social Welfare, XXV*(3).

Index

148